AURAS

AND HOW TO READ THEM

AURAS

AND HOW TO READ THEM

SARAH BARTLETT

COLLINS & BROWN

First published in Great Britain in 2000
by Collins & Brown Ltd
London House, Great Eastern Wharf,
Parkgate Road, London SW11 4NQ

Distributed in the United States and Canada by Sterling Publishing Co,
387 Park Avenue South, New York, NY 10016 USA

9 8 7 6 5 4 3 2 1

British Library Cataloguing-in-Publication Data:
A catalogue record for this book is available from the British Library.

ISBN 1-85585-746-4

Editorial Director Liz Dean
Design The Bridgewater Book Company
Cover design Alison Lee/The Bridgewater Book Company
Editor Lindsay McTeague

Colour reproduction by Classic Scan, Singapore
Printed and bound by New Interlitho, Italy

CONTENTS

INTRODUCTION

When I was a child I lived in the Far East. The existence of an aura emanating from every natural object was never doubted there, and those who were particularly gifted – those who had the ability to see the colours of the energy field radiating from anything from a person to a stone – were all considered healers. My amah, Lim Oo, was one such woman.

Although Lim Oo spoke very little English, together we managed to communicate and I discovered that she could see my aura. Every day she would 'read' my aura and tell me its colours, and sometimes she would question me, asking if I felt well, or happy, or sad. She would always nod wisely and smile her gold-capped teeth at me as if to confirm her own feelings or perceptions. For example, once when I became very ill, suffering from a malaria-like fever, she told me that my aura showed many areas of grey. When I recovered, she told me that it had returned to its vibrant orange, red and aquamarine; these colours are indicators of vitality, passion and creativity, common in the auras of young people and children.

I myself could not see the colours around anyone or anything so I began to try to force myself to see them, feeling sure that if Lim was able to see them, then so should I. However, the more I tried to see auras consciously, the more disillusioned I became, believing – like so many other people – that I was never going to be able to see them. It was only when I gave up determindedly trying to see auras and literally 'let go' that I began to sense auras in my own way. I had learned to use another, more subtle sense – the sixth sense, or intuition.

I began to experience the vibrations of someone's aura as they entered a room and, over time, I gradually began to link this heightened perception of their presence with the colour vibrations of their auras. I then understood that it was not so much the physical ability to see the colours of the aura that was important, but the ability to sense the aura vibrations in other subtle ways. I also came to appreciate the value of interpreting what you intuited, felt, saw, heard, smelled or touched, and how I could use that knowledge to help others. This is because auras reflect the state of your being – as the radiating force of your energy field, it reveals not only your personality, but your physical health and emotional well-being.

Most people in the West do not know what an aura is, and usually think of it as just a colourful cloud or rainbow surrounding the body. Historically and in contemporary art, the human aura has been depicted variously as a halo or as a series of coloured lights surrounding the head. Today, most people think that auras are only seen by psychics and clairvoyants, but the truth is that you don't actually have to physically 'see' the aura with your eyes. You can also experience or be aware of the aura – whether your own or someone else's – through using the other senses, those of sound, touch, smell and intuition.

This book is intended for anyone who wants to understand more about themselves and their relationships with other people. Reading auras is like reading your mood and your current state of being. Being able to interpret someone else's auric energy field means you are better able to understand that person, to know what makes them tick. It means you are able to relate to others with more compassion and tolerance. Knowing the current state of your own aura, of your life-force, means you can look at your lifestyle, career, health and also your relationships and work towards improving them or making changes, perhaps integrating certain aspects and qualities that may be lacking in your life.

USING THIS BOOK

In Western cultures, auras have long been considered as mysterious, spiritual and even – by sceptics – as figments of the imagination. This book examines some of the thinking on auras, from myths and legends to ancient healing practices and scientific facts that validate their existence. Modern scientific research shows that electromagnetic energy fields emanate from the human body, as well as every other living thing and also some inanimate objects. Thanks to the development of aura-imaging techniques, these can now be captured on camera, and it is possible to physically see the human aura.

Through a series of practical techniques and exercises explained in Chapter 2, this book shows you how to develop your senses of sight, sound, touch, smell and intuition to enable you to read someone's aura – whether your own or that of a friend. All that you need is to find your favourite way of perceiving the aura, along with the ability to interpret what you are experiencing. The Aura Workday Spa, for example, shows you how to practise sense development techniques during a normal day at work. None of these methods require specific skills, nor do you have to become psychic to 'see' the aura.

Chapter 3 looks at twenty of the colours most likely to be seen in the aura, giving a rundown of positive and negative traits that are associated with them, along with the most usual colour combinations. The chapter ends with examples of how to use this colour information to interpret auras. The aura gallery consists of a series of portraits taken using an aura-imaging camera, with an analysis alongside each one of what the various colours indicate. Turn to The Verdict pages to see how accurate the interpretations are. All the author had to work from was the aura photograph itself and the snapshot of each individual – she was given no additional information, such as the age or the occupation of the subject.

The link between aura colours and the other senses is explored in Chapter 4, which shows you how to discover an auric colour using keywords for the senses of hearing, touch, smell and intuition. Once you have found your current auric colour, you can turn to the pages that summarise your situation now – your lifestyle, your feelings, your thoughts, your work and your health – and the ways you can improve and develop certain qualities in your life.

Chapter 5 looks at auras and your relationships, suggesting that the types of people with whom you choose to become romantically involved may unconsciously be influenced by your auric colours – and theirs. To see if your current

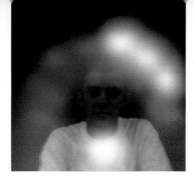

The human aura captured on camera appears as a series of coloured lights.

The aura is your personal energy, which consists of electromagnetic particles radiating from the body in several layers. This auric field is emitted from every living thing. It is your life-force and reflects all aspects of your body, mind and spirit — what you think, feel and experience in life.

The word 'aura' comes from the Greek word meaning 'breeze' or 'air'. It is this 'air' or energy that emanates from your body. This invisible energy also permeates rocks, mountains and inanimate objects; it breathes life into the world and is the universal energy and life-force of the cosmos. The Sun itself has an aura, as do the Earth and all the other planets. Look at the rings of Saturn, or the extraordinary clouds of gaseous energy around Jupiter. The Moon is said to have a special aura because when it is full it has an effect on animals such as wolves, which howl eerily. On still, cloudless nights you can see the Moon's haloed effect quite clearly.

This life energy that every living thing radiates can now be measured with special instruments and is usually revealed using photography or aura-imaging techniques (pages 16–17). The aura is both your personal life-force energy and your connection to other people's energy and their personal space. It also connects you to the greater universal energy of which everyone is a part. When you meet someone for the first time, you might have an immediate first impression of them. This is your unconscious recognition of their aura and your sense of how different from — or how similar to — their aura yours is.

WHAT IS THE AURA LIKE?

In art, an aura is often depicted as a halo. In fact, your aura is a reflection of you. Most people who have seen auras say they are like a rainbow of colours shimmering out from the body. The human aura is said to have seven layers. The first layer, closest to your skin, relates to health. The last, or outermost, layer relates to how you want to be seen by others and is also the spiritual layer. The aura is many-coloured and flows and moves with you, changing colour with your moods, feelings and sense of self. As they swirl around the body, some auras radiate out as far as a metre or two, others only several centimetres. Some people have multicoloured auras, others only one colour dominant.

In Eastern countries the source of auric energy is the *hara*, a place just below the navel. The auric field connects you to nature, to your 'gut' instinct, located in the centre of the stomach. You are not just a haloed head cut off from your body, you are bound inextricably to your complete state of being, gut instinct and all.

The special energy fields, known as chakras, at different points around the body are integral to the aura. They are gateways to sacred channels, receiving and sending out the energy that is your auric life-force. You can't see chakras, but you can sometimes feel the energy at points around the body. To activate your hand chakras, for example, rub the palms of your hands together for about one minute until you feel them tingling, then slowly separate your hands to experience the magnetic pull of the aura. For tips on how to awaken your chakra energy see pages 38–39.

HISTORY AND MYTH

Throughout history, almost every civilisation has acknowledged the existence of the aura, often using other names for it, including chi, prana, Karnaeem and Illiaster. The aura was described by Indian and Chinese mystics as long ago as 4000 BC. Some five thousand years later, Buddhists, Christians and Native Americans independently recorded the existence of the aura.

Practitioners of traditional Chinese medicine today still believe the force of this energy runs through the body along meridians, or pathways. By applying pressure to specific points on these meridians, the flow of vital energy through the body can be restored. According to Indian yoga and other spiritual and esoteric beliefs, the energy emanates from the seven chakras.

The interaction of colour and the human electrical field has also been important in the history of healing. The ancient Egyptians, in the sixth century BC, placed coloured stones and amulets at various energy centres on the body, a practice still employed today in crystal therapy to cure illness. At about the same time, Pythagoras, the Greek philosopher and mathematician, used musical vibrations and colour to heal people. In about 500 BC, in ancient Persia, a form of colour therapy was used for healing based on the light that radiated from the individual. By AD 1000, medicine was making great advances in the Arab world. Avicenna led the way with his *Canon of Medicine*, suggesting that the colour of a person's skin was an important diagnostic guide. He published the fact that the colour red increases blood circulation.

ART AND LITERATURE

In nature, the aurora is a luminous meteoric phenomenon with electrical qualities seen near both the North and South poles. The aurora borealis is seen in the high northern latitudes and its brilliant radiance in the night sky has inspired many myths. An Estonian legend suggests it is a wedding in the sky, with sledges, horses and thousands of guests who are all exuding the radiance of their own individual auras. Native American and Inuit peoples believed it to be the spirits of their ancestors at play.

Throughout the ages, many people have claimed to have seen auras. Perhaps among the most famous of these is the 16th-century French astrologer and physician Nostradamus, who is believed to have seen the aura of a monk. As a result of this sight, he predicted – correctly, as it eventually turned out – that the monk would one day be Pope Sixtus V.

For centuries, artists have tried to depict the aura, usually associated with religious or spiritual figures. Saints, the Virgin Mary and Jesus, Indian gods and the Buddha are most often depicted with a halo and sometimes light rays around the body. These are known as spiritual auras.

There are also many examples of auras in the Bible, including the brilliant light that shone around Saint Paul during his vision and conversion on the road to Damascus. A shining light 'darted' out from the face of Saint John of the Cross as he knelt in prayer, and Moses encountered dazzling lights when he descended from Mount Sinai with the Ten Commandments.

SCIENCE AND FACT

Despite the esoteric nature of auras, they have fascinated scientists and doctors alike for thousands of years, although they have also attracted their fair share of sceptics. With the development of ever-more sophisticated scientific methods as well as the revolutionary aura-imaging camera towards the end of the 20th century, there is now tangible physical proof of their existence.

Paracelsus, one of the key figures in medical science in 16th-century Switzerland, was a renowned physician and alchemist. Among his important works was his belief that a vital force, or energy, emanated from the human body, its radiation producing an envelope of light. He also believed that the quality of the light was the key to a person's state of health. Colours in the envelope of light were divided into two groups: those with a black hue represented illness and imbalance; those with a white hue represented harmony and wellbeing.

In the early 1800s, the Austrian physician Franz Anton Mesmer proposed that the universe was filled with a fluid – ether – which carried vibrations in its substance. He maintained that each living body had a direct influence upon other living bodies, transmitted through vibrations of the ether. Mesmer also confirmed the healing power of magnets and found that his own hands transmitted an energy that he termed animal magnetism.

In London in 1869, Dr Walter Kilner, who was fascinated by the claims of clairvoyants, began researching the human electrical field. He developed a basic detection device to make the aura visible to the human eye. Using dyes, a glass lens and screen he proved the aura could be seen and described what is now known as the physical aura – the first layer of the energy field. Later he identified the outer aura, or spiritual energy.

Biologist Alexander Gurwitsch, in 1923, discovered low levels of energy being given off by the plants he was studying. He called it mitogenetic energy. His work revealed the emission of a force field, which in esoteric circles was already known as an aura. At around the same time, a Cambridge biologist, Oscar Bagnall, became fascinated by Kilner's research and attempted to replicate the experiments himself. But he was not so successful and suggested that Kilner was probably also clairvoyant. He did, however, accept that all living things radiated an aura, and that the ability to see auric light did not depend on the focusing quality of the eye but on the field of peripheral vision.

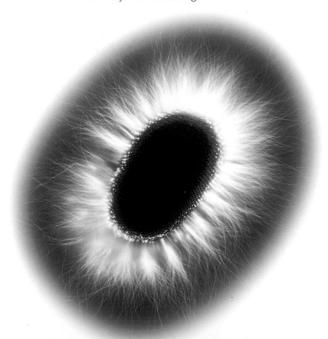

Kirlian photography reveals the magnetic force emanating from a fingertip.

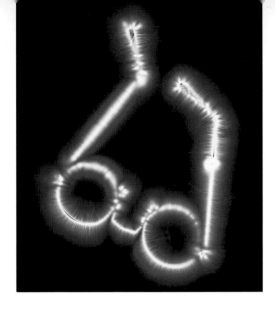

Even inanimate objects, such as these glasses, have an aura.

PHOTOGRAPHING THE AURA

The first person to succeed in taking photographs of the aura – in 1890 – was the inventor of modern electrical power, Croatian engineer Nikola Tesla. His earliest photographs were of the auras around the fingertips, but he later succeeded in capturing some around the entire body. His method involved attaching the subject's body to the photographic device with a large number of electrical wires.

In 1939, Soviet scientists Semyon and Valentina Kirlian developed Tesla's technology and came up with a more practical way of photographing the aura by using electrical plates that gave off a current. This method is still used today. The subject places their hand on the condensor plate and the electrical charge transfers from the plate to the fingertip and a photo is taken. When developed, the photo shows a coloured light extending from the fingertip.

By the 1970s, many researchers in the United States had become interested in the aura and turned their attention to providing scientific evidence of its existence. In 1980, an inventor called Guy Coggins developed a new technique, known as aura-imaging. It uses a special type of camera to produce a full spectrum of colours of the aura around the upper half of the body.

The aura-imaging system uses traditional biofeedback measuring techniques. According to Coggins, the camera does not actually see the aura, but perceives the light waves electronically, thus converting energy impulses into an auric image with the help of a computer. His first camera was a probe device that measured the aura by transmitting radio waves through the subject via a hand plate. The energy was received by a grid system behind the subject made up of a series of receivers and scanners, which processed the waves into electrical energy which was then transferred into colour and light.

Later, Coggins found an easier way to measure the energy impulses. He came up with a design that measures the same energy impulses directly from the hands, so the receiver system behind the subject was no longer necessary. The energy picked up by the probes is electronically converted into an aura image and recorded by the camera.

Using aura-imaging cameras has become an increasingly popular way of discovering what your own aura looks like at any given moment. However, as your mood and feelings change so do the colours of your aura, which means you may need to have your photo taken quite often to see if your aura picture changes. Coggins is now working on a new invention using a video camera to produce a full body video image in exactly the same way as the still camera. Based on the antennae grid design of his earliest invention, the video displays the aura as a moving field of colourful lights.

CHAPTER TWO

LEARNING TO SENSE AURAS

How many people do you know who make an impression just by being in the room? Film stars, actors, great leaders, politicians, and artists and writers are often dynamic, charismatic people. Charisma is about making a strong impact on other people, but it is also about a strong and powerful aura, which is the result of self-belief and self-awareness.

Even if you can't physically see a person's aura, you can
often sense it just by being in their company.

The aura was traditionally represented as a halo, often around a saintly head.

Since the aura reflects your individual personality, your success, as well as any change of mood or emotion, whatever energy you generate by virtue of being who you are — whether you're a quiet shy type or a self-confident extrovert — will be reflected in your aura.

Seeing an aura is not easy — how often have you 'seen' charisma? — but it does have a presence, just like a charismatic person. You can feel it in the air, or get a sense of excitement or awe in someone's presence, but you can't physically see it with your eyes. This is how you learn to read an aura, by using all the other senses and developing an instinctive feel for someone's aura, rather than trying to see rainbows, haloes and shimmering lights. By developing all your senses, you eventually discover that you are more likely to touch, intuitively feel or even smell a person's aura than see it.

SENSING AURAS IN OTHER WAYS

In the animal world, hearing, smell, touch and instinct are as important for the survival of the species as sight is. In fact, many animals rely on their nose and ears far more than on their eyes. Grazing antelope, for example, with their eyes at grass level, instinctively sense the presence of a predator by sound or smell long before they see their enemy.

Humans' sense of sight is conditioned to seeing objects so they can be named. Children may unknowingly see auras, but as their language skills develop they learn to label more and more things by sight. Rarely does anyone tell them that the name for the energy that emanates from the human body is an aura. If children were told this, it wouldn't be surprising to hear many of them exclaim, 'Hey, I can see your aura.'

As you grow older you lose your natural ability to be aware of someone's aura. This means you also, to some extent, start to lose touch with your senses, the most instinctive part of your nature. Sensing the invisible energy that interconnects everything becomes harder, simply because the more energies you are exposed to from external sources, the more trouble you have separating the 'good' vibrations from the not so good. With practice, however, you can learn how to tune into all your senses, which will help you to be able to hear, smell, feel and touch auras, as well as see them.

DEVELOPING THE OTHER SENSES

Apart from sight, which other senses come into play when you look at this picture? Can you sense the woman's tranquillity or do you want to touch the spiky flowers?

Initially, you may not be aware of auras at all. But by developing all of your senses, you can begin to experience other people's energy and become more conscious of what your own aura feels like. The aura can be seen, but it can also be heard, smelt, touched and 'felt'. Good auric sensing comes not just from relying on one sense alone but on them all.

The simplest way to begin is to choose the sense you are most comfortable with generally. For example, if when you first enter a room you find you notice the fragrant aroma of potpourri or a vase of flowers, or perhaps the earthy smell of ethnic cushion covers, you should concentrate on your sense of smell first. If, however, your initial impression is of a ticking clock, the hum of a computer or gentle background music, your primary focus should be your sense of hearing.

The rest of this chapter deals with each of the senses individually, suggesting techniques and exercises for enhancing each one. When you are familiar with the exercises, try to include them in your daily routine, and occasionally resolve to devote a whole day to developing your senses, as described in the Aura Workday Spa (pages 42–45). As well as strengthening and developing your own aura awareness, you can practise sensing the auras of colleagues and friends. You can also adapt the techniques to try at home over the weekend.

COLOUR VIBRATION

By developing your awareness of all the senses, you will be able to discover what is known as the colour vibration of your aura, as well as that of other people. The colour vibration of your aura is the colour that shows up in aura-imaging photography (see page 17). You can find out which is your most powerful auric colour without actually having to see it or have a photograph taken.

Each of the other senses apart from sight – smell, touch, hearing and intuition – can detect and identify the frequency spectrum to which the auric colours vibrate. For example, a specific kind of smell signifies the colour vibration for red, another kind of smell signifies the colour vibration for blue, another for yellow and so on. Similarly, each colour in the aura resonates to a particular type of sound. Finding out your current predominant aura colour can tell you everything about yourself, from your fears, skills, talents and spiritual awareness to your emotions, relationships and health. Remember, you don't literally have to 'see' the colour to find out the colour vibration of your aura. For more about relating individual colours to the senses, see chapter four, but only do so when you have developed your other senses and had a chance to practise using them.

DEVELOPING YOUR
SENSE OF HEARING

Detecting the aura through the natural vibrations of sound is just as valid as accessing it through the power of sight. Developing your sense of hearing to attune yourself to different messages sounded out from the aura can also be of assistance in interpreting the sounds.

Sound travels in waves caused by vibrations of the gas molecules that make up air. It cannot travel through a vacuum. The frequency, or pitch, of sound is measured in hertz, or waves per second. Humans can hear sounds in the frequency range from 20 to 20,000 hertz. Bats can hear much higher sounds, or ultrasounds, up to 200,000 hertz; birds can hear lower ones, or infrasounds. Because bats are nocturnal animals and cannot see well, they use echolocation to find their way. They emit high-pitched, ultrasonic sounds and listen for the echo reflecting off objects in front of them. They can work out how far away the object is by the length of time it takes for the echo to return to them.

The natural frequency of an object is the frequency at which it will vibrate freely. If a frequency that is the same as the natural frequency is applied to the object, the vibrations may become more intense, a phenomenon known as resonance. Thus a troop of soldiers marching in step over a bridge – even a sturdy one – could cause it to resonate and vibrate violently if the frequency of their footsteps matched that of the bridge. In a freak accident in the United States in 1940, resonance caused the Tacoma Narrows bridge to collapse when the frequency of the wind happened to coincide with the natural frequency of the bridge. On a smaller scale, a glass will shatter when a singer's voice resonates at the right frequency.

In terms of sound imagery, people use phrases like, 'We resonate so well' or 'He's got good vibes'. When you listen to people's voices, some sound grating, others beautiful and yet others sensual. This totally depends on your personal value judgements of the quality of the sound. What to you is a terrible noise – a sound you don't like – may well be music to another person's ears. Similarly, your voice frequency changes depending on who you are with, or on whose voice resonates harmoniously with yours.

The idea of hearing an aura may sound absurd, but if – like bats – people send out their own type of echo-sounding waves, then the quality of the voice at the end of the phone can give you a clue to a person's aura, just as if you were face to face with them. You can sometimes 'hear' mistrust, suspicion, deceit or humour in someone's voice before you can sense it in other ways. You might say, 'I don't like the sound of that!', referring not so much to the words that are spoken but to the intention or purpose behind the words.

Listening to the different qualities of voices on the telephone can develop your sense of hearing, so you can literally 'hear' someone's aura.

TECHNIQUES AND EXERCISES

By beginning to sense the quality of what you are hearing, even if it is simply a voice – your friend's or your own – you can get a sense of what the aura is reflecting. Each resonance reflects an auric colour. Try to be aware of what you are hearing and, more importantly, how you perceive the sound or person.

1 MUSICAL NOTES

Pluck or play a musical instrument and decide whether you like the sounds and why. Alternatively, listen to some of your favourite music and then to music you really detest. Think about why you like some sounds and consider others to be a noise.

2 BABBLING VOICES

In a crowded place, such as a café or airport, try to pick out one voice in the crowd. Decide why it is more powerful than others, or more interesting. Does it resonate with something you like or don't like in your own life? For
example, does it remind you of the soothing lilt of an actress reading a story on tape or of the strident tones of a boss who is always shouting at you?

3 SOUNDS OF SILENCE

Try to listen to the sounds coming out of silence. Sit quietly in a library, in your room at night, in a country lane or at the top of a mountain, and you will still hear sounds, however quiet you think it is. You are not living in a vacuum.

4 IN CONVERSATION

Have conversations with friends, colleagues and your partner. Listen to your voice and what it sounds like, what you are expressing behind the words. Do other people's voices get on your nerves – are they too high, too low, too sexy, too intimidating? Which voices do you love, which voices in the opposite sex turn you on? What do other people's voices seem to be expressing behind the words?

DEVELOPING YOUR
SENSE OF TOUCH

Touch is literally the most tangible of the senses, simply because as soon as you are in contact with a surface you take in all kinds of signals and vibrations, messages and reactions, which are relayed via the nervous system to the brain for interpretation. Depending on how sensitive you are to touch, you may know as soon as you shake hands with, or kiss, someone affectionately exactly how they truly feel.

Some people hate being touched because it means others are too close to their personal space or are invading their auric field. Other people love to be touched and often spontaneously put out their fingers to touch another person on the arm in friendship as they talk. Yet other people jump in alarm if a tiny spider crawls across their leg, while others still, brushing past a nettle, find the sting both pleasurable and irritating. Roman soldiers used to brush stinging nettles across their bare skin in cold weather to increase their blood circulation and keep them warm. The nettle sting caused the mind to register irritation on the skin but at the same time had the effect of warming the physical body.

Touch is the most basic sensual quality in relationships, from caressing a lover to dabbing the tears from a child's cheeks or giving a friend a massage. The word is also used to describe the emotive feeling of being touched by someone's generosity or sadness. Touch goes deeply into your sense of being and is one of the most physical ways of attuning yourself to the aura. Touching the energy of a leaf, a lover's aura, or feeling the power of your own chakra points is a vibrant and meaningful experience.

Stroking a cat is such a tactile experience that it always seems to give pleasure.

TECHNIQUES AND EXERCISES

1 NATURAL ENERGY

Place a leaf, a piece of fruit or a crystal in the palm of your hand. (All these natural objects have their own energy fields, their own auric properties.) Sit quietly with the leaf, or other natural object, in your hand and make sure you touch it with your fingers or thumb as well as feeling it on your palm. Sit back, close your eyes and concentrate on the leaf. As you do so, clear your mind and concentrate on what the leaf feels like in your hand. You may need to sit for several minutes – even up to 20 – depending on your own defences and in-built resistance to sensing the aura.

What does it feel like: warm, cold, electric, smooth, rippled, stimulating, vibrant? Does it make you feel angry, content, happy, sad, restless? Whatever energy you receive also depends on your own mood and auric field, which will be a channel for the aura of the object in your hand. Try this with various items before you move on to the next exercise. Experiment with personal items such as a favourite crystal, photograph or book which, as well as having their own aura, have become imbued with your own aura over time.

WATER TOUCHING

This simple exercise allows you to become quickly aware of a very different quality of feeling that is not solid to the touch. Fill a basin with water, run a bath or sit beside

a quiet pool or river where you can touch the surface with your fingertips. Now close your eyes. As you touch the water don't let your fingers sink below the surface, just keep them on the top like a water-boatman gliding across the surface. Think about what this touch means to you. Do you find it tranquil, smooth, soothing and silky or is it cold, shivery or barely perceptible?

Touching something that is not usually touched, such as water, and focusing on the sensations you feel, is a good exercise.

3 TOUCHING THE AURIC FIELD

You need two people for this exercise. Stand facing each other and slowly raise your hands towards each other, but don't ever touch. Keep your hands about 15 cm (6 inches) apart, then close your eyes and concentrate on the energy you are receiving and the energy you are giving out. Only do this for a few minutes at a time or your arms will get tired. Try and touch what the other person's aura is telling you. For example, is it warm, electric, rough, textured, bristly, shaggy, soft, unruffled? Does it make you feel welcome, tense, angry or vitalised?

Next take turns receiving and giving energy. Simply open yourself to the other person's energy and drop your protective auric screen. Everyone builds up a resistance to difficult energy, but some more so than others, which means you can't always sense what your own aura is really like, let alone anyone else's. When it is your turn to give energy out, imagine the flow of energy beginning from the hara, just below your navel. As the energy radiates through your body, breathe deeply and imagine the force passing out through your hands towards the other person.

4 AURIC EMBRACE

You need a friend or partner for this technique, but make sure you have tried the giving and receiving of energy in the last exercise before you try it. Stand facing each other with just enough space between you that you are not touching or making contact at any point on your bodies. Close your eyes, relax and breathe deeply. Put your arms around your friend as if to embrace or hug them but don't actually touch their body. Hold your arms like for this for about 30 seconds, or longer if you can, and begin to sense their energy field with your hands. Make sure your friend does the same to you afterwards to restore the balance of energies.

5 AURIC MASSAGE

You can do this to yourself on a small scale, but it is much better to get a friend or partner to do it to you and vice versa for deeper awareness. Ask your friend to lie on their back on the floor or a firm surface, with their eyes closed. Now begin your massage. Without making contact with the body, place your hands over their head and gradually move them over all areas of the body as if you were giving them a real massage. Keep your fingers together and go slowly and gradually in a sweeping movement from side to side as you move down the body. The massage should last about two to three minutes. Your friend should feel the benefits of this technique as your energies connect, and you may well find that you can feel their auric field. If you do, try to think what it feels like. Is it soft, gentle, silky and smooth, or crisp, ruffled, bumpy and cold? Now get your friend to do the same to you, and you will feel your own aura connecting with their hands.

Being aware of what things feel like means you are more able to sense the auric field that is given out by every living thing.

DEVELOPING YOUR
SENSE OF SMELL

Smell is perhaps the sense that is least thought about and there is a tendency to lump smells into two simple categories: either pleasant fragrances or unpleasant odours. It is also a very personal sense, with people having definite preferences; some opt for exotic, spicy aromas, while others prefer the more pungent smell of musk or fresher tang of citrus. Learning to 'smell out' people's auras means you are widening your awareness and opening yourself to more than just a visual reaction.

In the animal world, smell is often superior to the other senses, and not just in the wild. It is thought that dogs use their noses to sense their owners returning home from work up to 3 km (2 miles) away. Although humans do not have such acuity, according to a recent report in the *British Journal of Psychology*, your memory of past events improves if you connect smells to them at the time. For example, the smell of freshly baked bread may conjure up a memory of happy times playing at your grandparents' house.

Aromatherapy is beneficial to mind, body and spiritual awareness, using the power of fragrance to heal and cleanse the system and restore your sense of wellbeing. Some people are unaware of the power of their olfactory sense, which may in fact trigger a gut reaction.

For example, on entering a house that 'gives you the creeps', it may be that the house's aroma has induced the feeling, reminding you of something you instinctively know does not align with your personal sense of harmony.

Pregnant women find taste and smell changing throughout their pregnancy as their hormone levels fluctuate. Age, too, brings different likes and dislikes. Children instinctively like some scents and not others, whereas adults grow into more complicated aromas and fragrances, like strong cheeses or musky oils. The aromas you prefer are a benchmark of your current harmonic state and, therefore, the state of your aura (see pages 86–87). Developing your awareness of people's aromas is a way of sensing their aura just as if you were seeing it.

The fragrances you currently like indicate the state of your own aura. Choosing roses means you are probably in love.

Learning to smell effectively needs practice. It's about your awareness of your reactions as well as the quality you are sensing.

TECHNIQUES AND EXERCISES

1 *DEEP BREATHING*

First practise breathing deeply and rhythmically. This encourages good blood circulation so that your body and mind can integrate the smell as an image or idea. Sit with your legs crossed on the floor, or in a comfortable chair, and keep your back straight. As you breathe, close your eyes and count rhythmically. Count one as you inhale, then exhale; count two on the next in-breath, then exhale; and so on.

Next breathe and smell a pleasant fragrance. For example, as you inhale, imagine the smell of a rose; as you exhale, ask yourself what this scent means to you. Does it bring back a memory, invoke a feeling or convey a message to you about the rose?

2 *NOSE TRAINING*

Raid your larder, bathroom cabinet, fridge and dirty laundry for other fragrances and smells. Take a deep breath through your nose and allow the aroma to permeate your body, then as you exhale think about what the aroma evoked for you. Use items that include a good balance of sweet, sour and pungent, such as vinegar, honey, your favourite perfume, a rose or fragrant flower, an onion cut in half, a dirty sock (or other unpleasant smell), soap, lemon, garlic or mint. Decide what each of the smells in turn remind you of, whether you find them pleasant or unpleasant, and what it is about the smells that distinguishes some of them and not others. Which means the most to you and why?

3 *RECOGNISING SMELLS*

Try to do these two simple exercises every day. It only requires awareness and a little forethought and soon you'll be sniffing out everyone and everything. Recognising smells that convey certain messages soon becomes as natural as breathing.

First, take a deep whiff of air as you enter a new environment such as a shop or friend's house. Try to work out what the smell suggests to you. Second, each time you meet someone, take a deep – unobtrusive – breath and smell their presence. What do they smell of: cigarettes, perfume, sweat? Or can you smell something else? If so, what does it seem to convey to you: happiness, joy, boredom or maybe even success?

Following the spiral of the shell with your eyes is good training (see page 32).

DEVELOPING YOUR
SENSE OF SIGHT

Sight is the sense that most people associate with reading auras, but it is, in fact, the most difficult one to develop for this purpose. This is because people are conditioned to focus on objects and see in only a physical sense, with no emphasis on seeing the intuitive sense, as discussed on pages 36–39. Objective physical vision of the colours of the aura is possible, but it takes a lot of practice. You need to learn to train your eyes to recognize more and more of the light spectrum (see pages 46–47) and also become more aware of peripheral vision.

In humans, the field of view – what you can see to the side without moving your head – is about 120 degrees up and down and 200 degrees from side to side. Both eyes see the 120 degrees immediately in front of you, which enables you to perceive depth – the brain uses the overlapping images of left and right views to build up a three-dimensional picture. Each eye then has an individual field of vision of about 40 degrees to the side. Some animals, however, such as rabbits, can see behind them.

Our sense of sight is so important that 70 per cent of the sensory receptors are contained within the eyes. To enable you to see an object, light from it passes through the transparent cornea at the front of the eye and then through the pupil. The size of the pupil is adjusted according to the amount of light entering the eye by the muscular, coloured iris surrounding the pupil. This means that the interior of the eye receives a fairly constant amount of light. The light then passes through the lens, which helps the cornea to focus the light rays to form a clear upside-down image on the retina. This information passes to the brain, which interprets the image as being the right way up.

The retina contains two types of light-sensitive cells – rods and cones. Rod cells detect shades of black and white and are found mainly around the sides of the retina. Cone cells, positioned mostly in the centre of the retina, detect colour. Each one is sensitive to one of the three primary colours of light – red, blue or green – and triggers the release of a chemical to make you aware of the colour. Recent research has shown that the brain actually adds to the perception of the colour according to the brightness of surrounding objects and the contrasts between them. Thus colour is deduced as well as sensed. By doing exercises to stimulate your perception of colours and shadows you can improve your sight and peripheral vision. Only then will you begin to see the auric fields around plants, animals and people.

TECHNIQUES AND EXERCISES

Stimulate your eyes in preparation for seeing auras. First, perform a few simple exercises every day to increase your colour awareness and peripheral vision.

1 DEEP BREATHING

Sit quietly and breathe in deeply and slowly through your nose. Exhale through your mouth – a little faster than the in-breath – and feel the release of energy and any tension. Do this three or four times then breathe normally. Do this exercise before each of the sight improvement exercises that follow.

Above: Look at each of the dots on the dice in isolation to exercise your eyes (see right).

2 SPIRALLING SHELL

Look at the spiral in the shell (page 31) and stare at the centre of the spiral as if you were looking into a deep cave or well. Slowly allow your eyes to work their way out of the spiral, following the shell every bit of the way, until you reach the end. At first you may find your eyes want to jump out of the middle and move too fast, so keep practising a few times a day until you really feel you have followed the curve all the way from the centre to the end without cheating.

3 SEEING DOTS

To ensure your eyes develop better perception of light, shape and form, use this exercise daily and soon you will have faster eye reactions and movements than a hawk. On a piece of A4 paper, draw five black dots about 1 cm (3/4 inch) in diameter. Put one in each corner and one in the middle, like those on a dice. Stare at one of the black dots, then move your eyes quickly to the dot diagonally opposite, then quickly back to the dot you started with. Now move your eyes round all the dots using circular, diagonal or horizontal movements, for about ten seconds each time. Lastly, cover one eye and do the same exercise. Repeat using the other eye.

4 COLOUR IMPROVEMENT

All this exercise requires is for you to be observant as you stroll through the park, walk along the street or even sit in your garden. Try to see gradations within one colour. Separate different shades of green and see how many you can see or name. Do the same with the red spectrum, as well as the blues and yellows in nature. Look at the sky on a clear vibrant day and see how far you can see into the colour. Moonlit nights are particularly useful for distinguishing a new range of colours, and the softer focus and duller outlines of night vision also mean your level of awareness increases.

5 PERIPHERAL VISION

To increase your awareness of your peripheral vision, hold a finger out in front of you and stare at it for a minute or so. As you focus on your finger become aware of everything else around it, without actually focusing on anything else. Concentrate on your finger but know what else is in the room, gradually increasing your peripheral awareness by beginning to see out of the corners of your eyes as you look straight ahead. Be aware of the things that are going on almost behind you.

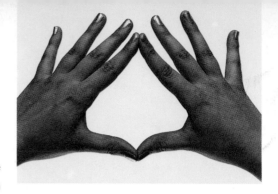

TECHNIQUES AND EXERCISES FOR SEEING AURAS

When you feel ready, perhaps after doing the previous exercises every day for a week, you can start trying to 'see' auras.

1 HUMAN AURA

Begin by practising holding your hands in an onion shape as shown right. Find a friend or partner to be your guinea pig. Ask them to stand in front of a white wall or, failing that, against a plain, unpatterned background. Raise your hands in an onion shape at arm's length in front of you and imagine the shape is a camera lens or telescope centred on your friend's body. Hold it up for a few minutes or for as long as you can without your arms tiring.

Concentrate on the image of your friend and still your mind. Then gradually, and very slowly, part your hands. Carry on concentrating and staring at your friend in the same spot. Do not look at your hands. As you move your hands slowly apart you may find that you begin to see the person's aura appear around their body, just for a moment. Practise this with other living things, like trees or animals. Like everything else, seeing auras depends on how receptive you are to opening all your senses.

2 CANDLE AURA

Sit quietly in a darkened room one evening and do the deep breathing exercise on page 32. Light a candle and place it in front of you on a table. Concentrate on the candle flame and watch it flicker and burn. The more still the flame the better. Focus for a few seconds on the flame and you will begin to see a glow with your peripheral vision. Try to imagine what the colours of the aura around the candle are. Don't do this for longer than a few seconds because it can tire your eyes.

3 YOUR OWN AURA

Sit in front of a mirror, preferably in the evening and when you are feeling relaxed. Make sure the lighting is dim and that you won't be interrupted. On a table or ledge immediately behind you place a lit candle that cannot be seen in the reflection as you look at yourself, but creates a glow around you as you stare into your face in the mirror.

Concentrate on your image and try to stare into your own eyes. Relax and listen to your breathing. Empty your mind of all thoughts by breathing as if you were meditating (see page 36). Depending on your own ability to sense the aura, it may take a few minutes before you begin to perceive the glow of the candle around you actually illuminating your own aura. Remember, you may only see the candle glow at first. It takes practice. This image will change according to your mood, so try the exercise again when you are in a different mood.

Once you know the candle is illuminating your aura, try the exercise without the candle. Concentrate on your image in the mirror and out of the corner of your eyes you may see and sense the radiance of your aura.

A person's smile is more than just a movement of the lips. Check to see whether joy is reflected in their whole face.

SMILING

Everyone's smile reveals the state of their aura. Look at your friends' smiles and see if you can work out what they are expressing with them – is it politeness, pleasure, enjoyment or true inner warmth?

Practise smiling at yourself in the mirror and notice the difference when you are smiling and not smiling. Practise smiling for different reasons. Smile because someone makes you laugh, smile because it's a beautiful day, smile because you intuitively feel connected to someone's chemistry. Look at everyone you meet in the corridor or in the street. When you feel brave, smile at them first and notice their own auric smile. Listen to laughter, too. Different laughs express different personalities. Everyone laughs and smiles, but not always with feeling – their lips might go through the motions even though their eyes do not light up. Try to look beyond the smile.

DEVELOPING YOUR
SENSE OF INTUITION

Often known as the sixth sense, intuition – also called gut instinct or even psychic awareness – is the key sense that tells you about the aura. The other senses – sight, sound, smell and touch – are all used to report back to your inner intuitive sense, the sense that interprets the signals you are receiving. By developing a better awareness of your intuitive sense you will find that reading auras becomes as natural as reading a book.

TECHNIQUES AND EXERCISES

1 *MEDITATION*

Open up your energy field with meditation techniques, which help you get closer to your inner voice and intuition. If you create a peaceful centre within yourself, when you start to intuit the feeling you are receiving from someone's aura, you will find that this inner space automatically sends a signal to your mind and interpretation becomes immediate. Being relaxed is valuable to both mind and body and also ensures that your own auric field is open and receptive.

Choose a quiet place and give yourself half an hour off from routine, the telephone and chores. Sit cross-legged on the floor if this is comfortable for you; if not, sit on a chair. Keeping your spine straight, rest your wrists on your knees and tuck your thumbs and middle fingers together to make a circle.

Close your eyes or focus on an image, crystal or point on the floor in front of you. Become aware of your breathing. As you inhale, try to let go of all thoughts except the awareness of your breath. As you exhale, begin to count. When you reach ten go back to one again to keep you focused. If you find your mind starts to wander begin at one again. If you find it impossible at first to meditate

Meditate somewhere peaceful, and empty your mind of all thoughts.

without your thoughts intruding, choose a mantra – a word or sentence – to repeat over and over again to block out your thoughts. After five minutes or so you may find your breathing is relaxed and easy, your body begins to feel totally calm and you have no thoughts or images in your mind. Only the awareness of every moment and the sounds or changes in the energy around you become more intensified. Listen to the silence.

When you feel ready to come out of your meditation, open your eyes or move your gaze from the object in front of you, take a deep breath and affirm to yourself that you are now open, relaxed and have inner peace.

2 VISUALIZATION TECHNIQUE

You can do this anywhere, on a bus, at work, walking down the street or sitting quietly alone. First relax and breathe quietly using the meditation technique above for a few minutes to ensure a deeper level of receptivity.

Close your eyes and imagine you are walking down a long road. Imagine where you have been, what you were doing before you reached this point on the road and why you are there. To your right are fields, rivers and a beautiful landscape, to your left is a huge cave in which you decide to rest for a while. In the cave is a golden mat and as you sit on the mat, a shimmering shaft of pure white laser light beams down on you through the roof of the cave. You close your eyes and as the shaft of light touches the top of your head, you feel the power of life-force energy entering your body. Imagine the light flowing through and round you, circling every muscle and organ and reaching into all your limbs, until you let it rest in the area below your navel, the hara. Your own life-force energy has been topped up. Now imagine it any colour you want it to be. If you feel inspired by blue, then imagine it to be blue; if you are feeling passionate about life, perhaps choose red. As you envisage the colour, think of it permeating every cell of your body and, as it does so, radiating through and beyond your body, not only in front of you but also behind you, to the sides, above and below.

Now you are surrounded by your own life-force energy and the cave is filled with your light and your aura. You stand up and walk out of the cave into the daylight. As you walk, the energy emanates from you and you now see your colour radiating around you. Imagine that further down the road you meet a friend who has been to their own secret cave; imagine what their aura looks like. Now imagine touching their auric field with your hands. What does it feel like, what colours can you see, what does this person smell like and what can you hear when they speak?

Now begin to draw back from your friend and take with you the image of their aura. As you turn away from your friend, and before you totally let go of the image, gently imagine your own aura resting now, but still radiating from your body. Slowly open your eyes and come back to reality.

Use this technique whenever you feel you need to vitalize your own aura, and also to increase your instinctive reactions and intuitive skills for reading auras.

CROWN CHAKRA
(ULTRAVIOLET)

THIRD EYE CHAKRA
(VIOLET)

THROAT CHAKRA
(BLUE)

HEART CHAKRA
(GREEN)

SOLAR PLEXUS CHAKRA
(YELLOW)

SAKRAL CHAKRA
(ORANGE)

ROOT, OR BASE, CHAKRA
(RED)

AWAKEN YOUR CHAKRA ENERGY

Many Eastern spiritual traditions maintain that a system of energy flows through the body linked by several energy centres, or chakras. There are seven main chakra energy centres (see left) and many minor ones – on the hands, feet, elbows and knees, for example. It is important to work with the primary chakras first. By developing an awareness of these threshold energy fields in yourself, you will begin to sense other people's chakras. Increase your chakra awareness by working with each of your chakras in turn.

Start with your root chakra. Sit comfortably on the floor and move your hands behind you to the base of the spine, palms facing in, without touching your body. As you hold your hands about 2.5–5 cm (1–2 inches) away from your body, you will feel the energy emanating from the root chakra. It may feel warm or solid. This area governs the kidneys, teeth, nail and bones.

Next move your hands slowly round and up to your sacral chakra. Hold them close together, fingertips touching, over the area below your navel, making sure your fingers are slightly cupped and there are no gaps. This chakra may feel watery, fluid and smooth, an indication of the fact that it governs the reproductive system, the pelvic area and the urinary system. Now move your hands slowly up to the solar plexus region, which usually feels warm and sometimes even fiery. This chakra governs the intestines, pancreas, liver and nervous system.

Move your hands over the heart chakra, where you will feel a lightness, warmth and mobility. It governs the circulation and the thymus gland. Keep aware of these key energy centres and the way you are reacting to them not just through your sense of touch but also through your sixth sense.

Now move your hands in turn over the chakras for the throat and third eye, which govern communication and intuition, respectively. Finally, when you reach the crown chakra, hold your hands over your head and feel the surging energy radiating from the area that is concerned with your higher spiritual self.

Once you have completed this exercise, you will begin to be able to sense other people's chakras and read whether they are relaxed or blocked, radiant or dull. It takes practice, but is essentially a vital connection to their whole auric field and its expression.

CHAKRAS, COLOURS AND HORMONES

Each chakra is associated with a particular colour in the spectrum (see left). The chakra points are also linked to glands within the body.

In 1989, research into the pineal gland in the brain revealed that it is physiologically linked to the hormone-producing glands in the rest of the body, and that these glands align exactly with the chakra points. The pineal gland releases the hormone melatonin, which may influence rhythms of activity. As your physical, emotional and mental states are changing all the time, so the colours in your aura change and the functions of the glands correspond with the energy functions and subsequent colour vibrations of the chakra points of the aura.

DREAMS AND AURAS

Working with dreams enables you to understand your moods, connect to your inner voice and open your intuitive channels. Your dreams reflect the state of your aura – and they tell you a lot about your unconscious world. Dreams and their meaning have been researched and studied by scientists and analysts throughout the 20th century. The great psychotherapists Jung, Adler and Freud all had a different approach to the interpretation of dreams, but they basically agreed that it is the symbolism of the dream that counts above all.

Doing some basic dream-work will make you more aware of your inner world and help you to develop your insight and intuition. The things that need to be made conscious in your life often form part of a dream; they can be as simple as dreaming of red roses or of falling over in the street. It is not the flowers or the fall in themselves that are important, but the meaning behind the images.

For example, as well as symbolising that you are deeply in love, full of joy and without a care in the world, dreaming of red roses may also be prompting you to acknowledge the importance of your relationship, both to yourself and your lover. Alternatively, you may be feeling nervous and worried about something you have to do at work, giving a presentation to a room full of important clients, perhaps. Your fear of failure, of 'tripping up', may express itself in your dream as the embarrassing situation of falling over, being out of control, in front of a whole lot of strangers. Once you are able to see beyond the literal representation and recognise what your dreams mean, you can take steps to deal with the situation. You could ask a colleague to listen to your presentation and offer constructive criticism, for example, or resolve to spend five minutes beforehand doing deep breathing exercises or a brief meditation (see pages 36–37) to help relax and focus your mind. If, however, your dreams are recurring or unpleasant, this may be a sign that there is a deeper issue that needs resolving or to be brought to light. Working out what the images or ideas behind your dream stories symbolise can help you discover your true values and needs.

KEEPING A DREAM JOURNAL

It is a good idea to keep a pencil and notebook beside your bed so that you can write down your dreams as soon as you wake up. Even if you wake in the middle of the night after a particularly vivid dream, you may find you have forgotten it in the morning if you don't immediately jot down the main aspects. Note any important events, colours or images that seemed to have meaning, as these can help you interpret your dreams.

Obviously, some kinds of dreams don't need analysing – they are usually dreams that are leftover remnants from the day before. You may wish to consult a dream therapist for an in-depth dream analysis, but you can put the work you have done on developing all your senses in this chapter to excellent use for some basic dream-work.

FEELINGS

Try to remember the feelings and sensations you may have felt in the dream. Were you happy or sad, anxious or carefree? Did you feel hot or cold, uncomfortable or relaxed? Again, write everything down as soon as you can and note how you felt when you woke up from the dream.

PEOPLE

Be aware of people, or types of people, who appear regularly in your dreams. Usually all these people, even if you know them in daily life, are just different aspects of you. If you are normally shy and introverted but constantly dream of a confident friend, this may indicate that you want to develop more of these traits yourself.

FREE ASSOCIATION

If you're not used to analysing dreams, try practising the art of free association. Start by using a simple image, for example, a cup on your desk. Immediately think of something associated with it – the first thing that comes into your mind – and then move on to further associations from there. You may think cup – tea – milk – cow – alpine meadows – avalanche. This helps you to see beyond an immediate symbol which is likely to be an unconscious indication of deeper feelings. The same principle applies in a dream. You've reached a crossroads and are looking at the signpost. The common symbolic association of this image is that you've reached a turning-point in your life – you have to make a decision or choice, perhaps, for example, about which

direction you need to take in your career, or where a relationship is going.

COLOURS

Familiarise yourself with what certain colours symbolise – use the free association method or the box below of some of the most common dream colours. If you do have colourful dreams, the chances are this will be reflected in the colours of your aura.

DREAM COLOURS

Red	You feel passion – love or hate – for someone.
Orange	You want to be noticed or to be the centre of attention. It's time to believe in yourself.
Bright yellow	You need to express your creativity or develop your talents.
Green	You have a positive attitude to life, a sign of inner healing.
Very dark blue/black	You are feeling low or depressed.
Light and bright blues	You are sensitive and intuitive.

AURA WORKDAY SPA

Every once in a while it is a good idea to dedicate a whole day to developing all your senses. The beauty of this aura spa day is that you don't have to take time off work for it, and no one need even know that you are doing it. Just follow the 'timetable' outlined below and adapt it to suit your own schedule.

ON WAKING

Open your eyes slowly and try not to focus on anything specific, become aware of what is happening around you. Your peripheral vision is at its most acute first thing in the morning, so take advantage and experience those things that aren't in focus but are in your field of vision. For example, what do you see as you gaze bleary-eyed in the mirror for the first time? As you pull back the curtains from the window and the light hits you, can you see the energy of the room suddenly come to life out of the corners of your eyes?

BEFORE BREAKFAST

If you have time, sit quietly for a few minutes and follow the basic principles of the meditation technique described on pages 36–37, which will prepare you for your day of auric awareness. The more relaxed and open you are to the world and life, the more likely you are to sense the aura of not just people, but plants and animals too.

BREAKFAST

As you pour your tea or coffee, make toast or eat yogurt or cereal, listen to the sounds you are making. Be really aware of the cups rattling on their saucers, the radio blaring, the milk gurgling into your cup, the kettle boiling. This increases your sound awareness and makes your hearing more acute. You also register certain vibrations you like the sound of, and those you don't like at all. As you eat, look at the colours of the food, the table, the clothes you are wearing and decide which ones you like and which ones you don't. Colour awareness is an important factor when interpreting the senses and reading auras, so get used to your personal choices in colour first.

GOING TO WORK

On your way to work, start developing your auric awareness of other people. If you travel by public transport you have an advantage as you are surrounded by others. For every person who comes into your auric space make a mental note of what it 'feels' like. You may still be unable to see an aura, but you will certainly by now have enough practice to take into account other sense reactions. Do they convey an air of confidence, a sense of arrogance, a feeling of sadness? What is it about their hair, or their smile, that makes you happy or feel uncomfortable?

If you drive to work by yourself, open the window enough for you to be able to hear some of the sounds outside. What does the traffic sound like? Is it noisy and impatient, punctuated by bursts of hooting and screeching brakes, or is it more of a constant rush of wind as cars speed by? Can you detect anything other than the noise of the traffic, perhaps birds singing or music from other cars? What do you like or dislike most about these sounds?

AT THE OFFICE

You'll be busy working, but keep your senses alert. If you use the phone all the time, listen to the voices at the other end of the line. What does the quality of the voices tell you, rather than the words? Notice any changes in the perfumes or deodorants your colleagues are wearing and try to define what kind of smell it is. This is the time of day when body rhythms are usually at their most concentrated, enabling you to focus clearly on ideas and be creative, so profit from this and test your auric powers.

RADIANT ENERGY

In your coffee break, ask a friend or colleague to try a simple aura test with you. As you approach the person, simply cup your hands and hold them out to them and try to 'feel' the energy radiating from their body.

PLANT ENERGY

Many offices have plants dotted about. If the state of the plants is not obvious at a glance, use your auric sense of touch to see whether they are alive and thriving or about to die. Cup your hands and hold them around the leaves or flowers. Do you feel heat, signalling that they are blooming; cold, which means they need attention; or simply nothing – they are almost dead?

BODY LANGUAGE

Practise observing body language. In those long meetings everyone ends up in at work, watch your colleagues and how they sit and talk. Are they aggressive, leaning forward on the table, or are they passive, preferring to sit back in the chair and make little contribution to the discussion? Do they gesticulate or find it difficult to communicate their thoughts? What do you think this tells you about the state of their moods, emotions or thoughts? Body language gives big clues to help you develop your power of intuition.

LUNCH AND AFTER

In the afternoon your perceptive qualities and rhythm take a dip, following normal body cycles, and this gives you an opportunity to cleanse and vitalize your own auric energy field, which has been soaking up everyone else's all day. Often people don't have the time to take a break for lunch and hurriedly eat a sandwich at their desks. If at all possible, try to get out of the office for a breath of fresh air. If you can't manage this, simply sit quietly at your desk for a few minutes without interruption.

To rejuvenate your aura, stand or sit comfortably and breathe slowly and deeply. Imagine a swirling diamond light shimmering towards you. As it draws closer imagine it embracing your body, completely enveloping you in its pure white light. Then imagine the energy gently massaging you, starting from your head and moving right down to your feet. As the energy passes over your body, try to imagine it purifying and vitalizing you. When the energy reaches the ground, let it leave your body.

Relaxing in a warm bath revitalizes your own auric energy after a tiring day.

GOING HOME

On your way home at the end of the day prepare yourself for a relaxing evening ahead. If you commute, try to keep poised and unflustered and not to use up valuable energy as you fight your way home. If your journey is long, you're probably generally tired and stressed, so avoid opening yourself to other people's energy fields, which may well be in the same depleted state as your own, as this can have a negative, draining effect. If you feel any unusual energy coming your way only allow yourself to open up to it if you are sure you are relaxed and objective about the message that is being sent out. Otherwise, concentrate on what you can hear, smell, see, and intuitively sense. What do other people's voices, aromas or body language tell you about them?

If you drive home, you can do the same routine as in the morning or perhaps put on one of your favourite tapes and try to pick out different instruments and analyse why you like or dislike their tone.

AT HOME

Devote the first hour or two after you get home (depending on how early it is) to de-stressing yourself. Run a warm bath, perhaps adding a fragrant bath oil, and practise the visualization technique on page 37. Then take a few minutes to consider what the water feels like against your skin. Is it soft, caressing and silky or hard and cold?

THE EVENING

When you prepare your dinner, be aware of the textures of different foods – the papery skin of onions, the firm smoothness of peppers, the velvety gills of mushrooms. Appreciate the different colours, too. Once you start cooking, enjoy the aromas and try to recall past events, people or memories that have some connection with these smells.

If you are eating in a restaurant, you can check out the auras of friends, other diners and the waiters by using your favourite sense, or a combination of all five. What does the waiter smell of? Is it just cooking aromas or does he convey his own spicy scent? Does your friend seem to radiate happiness, or does she seem aloof and worried? Do the strangers at the next table sound loud and noisy or are their voices quiet, discreet and soft? In each case, what do you think your impressions tell you about the people concerned?

If you are having a quiet evening in, try some peripheral vision exercises (page 33) and then perhaps attempt to see a candle's aura or even your own (page 34). If you are with a friend

you can try to see their aura using the 'onion shape' (page 34).

READY FOR BED

Before you go to sleep, lie or sit quietly and close your eyes. Breathe deeply and empty your mind of all thoughts, concentrating only on your in- and out-breaths. Once you feel relaxed, think about all the impressions and feelings you have had through the day. Which people gave you strong impressions, what did they seem to convey and how did you react to their presence? Which senses did you find easiest to use, and was your own aura energized by the presence of other people or did you feel uncomfortable or threatened? Asking yourself these questions is important to determine exactly how well you are doing with developing your senses.

As you drift off to sleep say to yourself: 'I love my aura. My aura is balanced and whole and is an expression of who I am.' Affirming your own aura means you can begin to understand other people's auras too.

In bed, take a few minutes to consider your feelings about, and impressions of, people during the day.

CHAPTER THREE
THE AURA AND COLOUR

The colours of your aura are vibrations of energy, swirling lights of particles that are given off from the electromagnetic charge of your energy field. According to quantum physics, everything in the known universe is made up of energy vibrations, whether it's your body or still water in a glass. These vibrations form waves, which together make up the electromagnetic spectrum. It includes radio waves, infrared radiation, visible light, ultraviolet radiation, X-rays and gamma rays. The distance between the crests of successive waves is the wavelength and the number of waves per second is the frequency. The longer the wavelength, the lower the frequency.

The colours humans are able to see range in vibration from lowest to highest – red, orange, yellow, green, blue, indigo, violet and ultraviolet. Thus red light has the longest wave-length and lowest frequency, ultraviolet the shortest wave-length and the highest frequency in the visible spectrum. The aura's frequency level is just beyond the range of light the human eye is used to seeing, but when captured on camera, or when literally 'seen' by the human eye trained to perceive a wider spectrum of light, these vibrations reveal a complete spectrum of colour.

Over thousands of years, colour has come to have certain characteristics associated with it. Colours are guides to the general picture of you and also to the state of your aura. People with strong intuitive skills can see the colours merging and changing depending on a person's current holistic state; they can also see if one colour is more dominant in the aura than others.

Each colour in the aura corresponds to a certain quality that reflects your personality, moods and feelings. Once you get to know more about what the colours represent, you can interpret the different qualities of each of the other senses. Each sense has ten specific different qualities, which correspond to the ten basic colours that are formed from combinations of the visible spectrum (see opposite). By using your other senses you can discover which colour is currently dominant in your own or another person's aura without having to see it (see pages 80–91).

COLOUR AND YOU

Think about the colours you like in your home and which ones you prefer to wear. Look at which colours other people prefer – their choice of colours for both clothes and interior decoration will tell you a great deal about their personality. How you feel about certain colours also tells you about yourself. The general rule is that if a colour makes you feel good, it is a colour or related quality you need to bring into your life at the time.

The following 20 colours (pages 48–67) are an indication of the innumerable shades and hues of the colour spectrum. These are the ones most likely to be seen in the aura, although there are many more. (When it comes to interpreting your own aura in chapter four only the ten basic colours have been used to keep it simple.) Remember when you start interpreting colours that each person perceives the world from their own sense of reality. Your auric colours are individual and you display these colours differently from other people. Treat the following interpretations as a general guide only.

When you are first learning to read auras, focus on the positive traits associated with each colour. Once you are experienced, you will be able to take the so-called negative traits into account. Generally speaking, these tend to be an exaggerated form of the positive traits and, because they are emphasised, may lead to an imbalance in your life. Some colour combinations occur more frequently than others in the aura. For the ones given on the following pages, the interpretation assumes that the first colour is more prominent than the second one. The reading will vary depending on the balance of colours, which may occur anywhere in the aura – they do not have to be adjacent. Thus a person with blue and red in the aura – that is, more blue than red – may have a different reading from someone with red and blue.

THE TEN BASIC COLOURS

Violet	Spiritual growth, imagination
Lavender	The magical, light-heartedness
Turquoise	Inspiration, ideals
Blue	Intuition, sensitivity
Aquamarine	Freedom, compassion
Deep green	Growth, balance, ambition
Yellow	Excitement, optimism, mental clarity
Orange	Creativity, originality, motivation
Pink	Tenderness, romantic love, longing
Red	Power, challenge, passion, action

ULTRAVIOLET

POSITIVE TRAITS

When ultraviolet is a strong vibrational colour in the aura it suggests inspiration, visions and dreams. It often denotes a powerful psychic ability. The person may not be aware of this gift if they are not normally able to use their psychic powers, but this is an excellent period to develop or make use of these skills. If the person learns to channel this powerful force, others will be astounded by their clairvoyant ability or amazing insight. This colour usually shows in highly creative and inventive people, and indicates originality and eccentricity.

NEGATIVE TRAITS

This colour can indicate that the person is under pressure. Being creative or artistic in any way is important for the person with ultraviolet prominent in their aura. It represents visions and dreams that are taking shape, as well as the ability to ground the inner awareness of a psychic sense. This kind of genius energy must have some channel or outlet otherwise it can cause a build-up of stress.

COMMON COMBINATIONS

Ultraviolet and orange

This combination often occurs in people who are highly creative – designers, artists and poets, for example. But they are people who also love having a joyful time. It is not a colour combination associated with loners.

Ultraviolet and yellow

These colours indicate a need to socialise and enjoy the fun side of life, to avoid stress and pressure from external sources. Goals must be original and creative, and these people need plenty of social interaction and entertainment from which to develop their skills and draw inspiration.

Ultraviolet and turquoise

This is often a combination seen in people who are in a 'healing' phase of their life. They need to be alone, but also find it easy to nurture others with compassion and deep psychic awareness. They need time to work on themselves as well as on others. Counsellors and nurses frequently display these two colours.

VIOLET

POSITIVE TRAITS

This colour usually represents the ethereal and the magical. When it is dominant in an aura it usually signifies the person's ability to find a deep spiritual purpose in their existence, as well as revealing a sense of humility and acceptance of life's difficulties. Vision and clairvoyance are also indicated. Violet represents a powerful imagination, as well as spontaneity and originality verging on the eccentric. It is also associated with genuine gurus and the ability to align the mind, body and spirit, while maintaining a sense of the transcendent nature of things.

NEGATIVE TRAITS

Someone with violet in their aura can become too attached to the spiritual world and start to live like a hermit, unwilling to enjoy ordinary pleasure and retreating into the world of religion or spirituality to escape reality. It can also show up in the aura when someone is oversensitive and emotional, or longing to escape into their dream world. It can suggest an introvert who prefers fantasy to reality.

COMMON COMBINATIONS

Violet and red

This combination is often found in charismatic individuals, such as actors, leaders and gurus, all of whom have a powerful presence expressed as a mixture of dynamic creativity and belief in their vocation. It frequently occurs when people are aware of their purpose in life, passion aroused by insight and awareness.

Violet and light blue

Sensitive people, mediums and clairvoyants display these two colours. Although it is a good combination for heightened awareness of the feelings of others, it can drain the individual's own feeling nature. There may be an inner struggle between empathy and a deeper need for escape from the overflow of energy.

Violet and green

This powerful combination indicates the ability to use the imagination and ground it in reality. It signifies a practical idealist – one who knows how to create magical worlds, either in fiction or fact, for the benefit of many. These colours are typically seen together in the auras of spiritual leaders and film directors.

INDIGO

POSITIVE TRAITS

This colour usually indicates psychic ability, coupled with an enthusiasm for mystery and magic. It represents the imagined world, and also a spiritual one. Generally, it marks a period of time when contemplation and reflection about the future are of deep significance. A profound and deeply spiritual awakening is also often indicated by indigo, and if it appears to dominate the aura then it suggests the person wants to escape from the mundaneness of everyday life and find a new and magical existence.

NEGATIVE TRAITS

Indigo can suggest an overt need for spiritual enlightenment or an obsessive desire for psychic contact. It can indicate a person who still cannot find a belief system or inner truth and relies heavily on the psychic powers of others in order to obtain answers.

COMMON COMBINATIONS

Indigo and green

Determination to succeed and a gentle spiritual awareness are the hallmarks of this combination. It is often seen in people who are organised and generous in the time they give to others. They may be ambitious but are not self-centred. They care for the environment and nature and are often involved in charity work or ecological issues – they are gentle aggressors.

Indigo and white

Together, indigo and white represent a need for a spiritual love. They are often seen in people who have found their soulmate or have devoted themselves to a spiritual leader or religion.

Indigo and pink

These two colours often show when people first fall in love. There is the idealism and belief of having found the perfect love, as well as the naivety of being blind to the reality of what love is really about.

LAVENDER

POSITIVE TRAITS

When this colour is prominent in the aura it usually indicates that reality and worldly affairs are of little or no importance to the person right now. Lavender represents reflection, meditation and healing. It indicates a need for harmony and peace, a quiet time to take a break from the rat race or daily routines and rituals. There is an almost magical quality about the person who has this colour dominant in their aura; they exude an ethereal charisma and are often happiest when living in the world of their imagination.

NEGATIVE TRAITS

The downside of lavender is that the person can become too attached to their imagination and dreams. There is often a tendency to withdraw totally from the realities of day-to-day living, as well as an almost cheeky desire to keep people guessing about their true motives.

COMMON COMBINATIONS

Lavender and red

When lavender and red occur together, this indicates a passionate imagination. The combination often shows up in people who are exhausting to be with because they are dynamic and inspiring about anything unworldly, but are rarely able to ground their ideas and dreams. They live with their head in the clouds, have magnificent visions and schemes but are unable to be practical.

Lavender and yellow

This combination often shows up in people who are childlike and enthusiastic about life. They never seem to have any worries or cares and are generally free of compulsions or anxiety. They live life to the full, seeming to radiate joy and introduce playfulness into everything they do and say.

Lavender and amber

These colours together indicate an intellectual approach to healing others and a curiosity to know what makes others tick. They are often seen in the auras of psychotherapists or people embarking on study of the arts or intellectually demanding courses.

DARK BLUE

POSITIVE TRAITS

This colour is usually an indicator of a strong and powerful sense of being. It represents sound judgement, honesty and reliability, and is the colour of steady, risk-free progress. Dark blue often occurs in the auras of enterprising business executives, who know exactly where they are going; they have ambition, but are also sensitive to the needs of others. It is also associated with peace and tranquillity, as well as periods of good fortune and harmonious living. When blue is dominant it indicates a time when feelings flow freely and the person connects to friends and colleagues with understanding and emotional integrity.

NEGATIVE TRAITS

Dark blue can signal a period when the mind has taken over from the feelings, with a subsequent overload of thoughts and plans. Meditation, exercise and active self-healing can be particularly helpful. This is a time for trying to reconnect with the feelings. Mentally, the person feels stressed and isn't ready to take on any more responsibilities or commitments.

COMMON COMBINATIONS

Dark blue and yellow

This combination indicates a period of optimism for the future and the ability to make sound and shrewd judgements. It is a good time to seize new opportunities. People with this combination need to sort out their priorities, deciding what is of emotional value to them and what is not.

Dark blue and deep green

When work and ambition are crucial, dark blue and deep green often appear together. They suggest extreme tension and stress, an overworked mind and the need to find time to relax away from the rat race.

Dark blue and light red

Those who feel passionate about their future — when there are promotion prospects or they are excited about a change in lifestyle — display this combination in their aura. It can also appear when they are deeply involved in a relationship and feelings are flowing beautifully.

SKY BLUE

POSITIVE TRAITS

Sensitivity and imagination are the qualities associated with this colour. It is often seen in the auras of artists, writers, actors and others in the creative professions, who have a well-developed imagination and – sometimes – their head in the clouds, in the sky. Sky blue is a sign of a strong gut instinct and, if blended with other shades of blue, indicates powerful intuition, although the person may not even be aware of possessing this quality. The colour can also imply that the person is going through a period when they are deeply in tune with everyone around them.

NEGATIVE TRAITS

The negative connotation of sky blue is that it can suggest a period of having to adjust to the world, perhaps a time of insecurity and self-doubt. If it is a dominant colour in the aura it can indicate someone who is immature and won't come down to earth. It is also a sign of a person being too compromising or too ready to listen to the opinions of others rather than formulating their own. When someone is going through a relationship break-up sky blue often appears in the aura.

COMMON COMBINATIONS

Sky blue and orange

Vitality and overexcitement are common with this combination. There is nervousness and a desire for intense communication and interaction, as well as a need to use a powerful imagination. Leaders and politicians often have this combination of colours because the positive aspect of blue adds insight and gut instinct to the extrovert nature of orange. In other people, it suggests they can't help but express themselves creatively and energetically.

Sky blue and pink

People who have fallen in love often exhibit sky blue and pink. This is a combination of sensitivity and infatuation, love and childlike desires. It may also indicate someone blindly falling in love with love, or imagining another person to be in love with them when they might not be. These colours often occur together when people are flirting or being seductive.

AQUAMARINE

POSITIVE TRAITS

This colour is always associated with compassion and affection. Because it crosses both the blue spectrum and the green, it is a dual colour. It is sensitive and refined, imaginative and gentle, but also organised and deliberate, motivated and sensible. It often appears in the auras of people who use their healing or compassionate nature in the workplace. Aquamarine indicates good health and a balanced and sincere nature; it is also a sign of an altruistic approach to life – everyone is equal, and personal freedom is of great importance. Typically, people with this colour in their aura know how to develop other people's skills and are able to encourage and support their friends and partners.

NEGATIVE TRAITS

When this colour is dominant in the aura it can represent a need for change or transition, a move away from a sensitive and secretive period towards a more organised and hard-working extrovert period. Other people often turn to those with aquamarine strong in their aura and expect too much from them, causing them to feel trapped and retreat.

COMMON COMBINATIONS

Aquamarine and red

This combination is associated with passion, creativity and motivation. There is devotion to a cause, or a need to join forces with someone else to create a better situation than existed before. It's a combination signalling optimism and determination to achieve, often seen in the auras of successful people who are original, creative and yet able to put their ideas into practice.

Aquamarine and yellow

A sense of fun and a warm-hearted nature are the hallmarks of this combination. It is found in people who are serious about achieving their objectives but are also able to let their hair down and are great fun to have around. They are lively and stimulating, both intellectually and spiritually.

TURQUOISE

POSITIVE TRAITS

This colour represents a positive attitude to oneself and one's needs. There is a firm but gentle approach to helping others. If turquoise is dominant in the aura, then energy levels are high and physical exercise is important. The person conveys a sense of peace and tranquillity, which other people often benefit from more than the person concerned. This colour often occurs in the aura when the person feels at ease and comfortable in other people's company and can relax and enjoy a peaceful atmosphere.

NEGATIVE TRAITS

If turquoise is constantly dominant in the aura it can indicate an obsession with the self, or a desperate need to be something or somebody in the world. The person is often unaware of their need to achieve success.

COMMON COMBINATIONS

Turquoise and terracotta
People who fight against convention, those with a rebellious nature or radical ways of thinking that will drastically change the way they see the world, often display this combination in their aura. There is something unusual or eccentric about people with these colours dominant, and they are usually inventive and self-absorbed, yet warm-hearted.

Turquoise and pink
This combination often occurs in the aura when people are in love. It indicates romantic longing or yearning and a sense of tranquil and heady spiritual love, rather than passion and a wild affair. Turquoise and pink are found in people who are infatuated or who have become involved in a project or with a person.

DEEP GREEN

POSITIVE TRAITS

This is the colour of reliability and genuine friendliness. The stronger the green, the greater the likelihood that the person is confident and going through a period of achievement and attainment. Deep green usually suggests a calm and unflappable personality, someone who is able to help others in a crisis without getting into a panic themselves. The person with a deep green aura, being grounded and down-to-earth in the truest sense of the world, is often happiest close to nature. But with common sense and a shrewd and pragmatic mind, they can achieve recognition in business or any field they choose.

NEGATIVE TRAITS

There may be a tendency not to take time to relax or give the body a chance to be revitalized. When deep green is highly dominant in the aura, the person may be experiencing such a powerful desire to achieve and succeed at work that they've forgotten about the more personal aspects of themselves – feelings, health and bodily needs.

COMMON COMBINATIONS

Deep green and sky blue

Those who can remain true to their feelings and sensitivity, yet also work to schedules and tight deadlines often display this combination. It is a sign that they can put their imaginative ideas into practice.

Deep green and red

This combination often occurs in the auras of successful people. Leaders, politicians, business executives and company heads usually have these colours in their aura. Passion, persuasion and communication skills are coupled with practical and down-to-earth realism. These are people who take risks, but make sure they check all the options first.

LIGHT GREEN

POSITIVE TRAITS

Initiative and the ability to make progress are the qualities associated with this colour. It is often seen in the auras of financially successful people or those who deal with money. When a person receives a salary rise or a bonus, light green often appears in the aura. Like dark green, light green also suggests a down-to-earth and often practical nature, but there is usually a lighter, less serious side to the personality, creating an almost airy feeling when the person enters the room.

NEGATIVE TRAITS

The only downside of light green is that people may become too eager to please everyone else, smiling and agreeing with everything that is said, that they don't really know what truly pleases themselves any more. They can be so practical and complacent about life that they don't ever think about what they are saying, or why they are doing what they do.

COMMON COMBINATIONS

Light green and sky blue

When these colours are together there is a high level of artistic talent and sensitivity to the surroundings, so the combination is usually associated with writers, artists, musicians and craftsmen. It is often seen in people when they are feeling inspired and enlightened about their future. This is a period when people can make good progress towards achieving their aims, and suggests clear thinking and clarity of vision. However, it doesn't necessarily imply that the work will ever get done. This is about inspiration, not practicalities.

Light green and yellow

Often seen in the aura when people are communicating and enjoying themselves, light green and yellow are typically found together in sporty types and livewires. They feel a need to get moving, to chatter incessantly or even to strike up conversations with strangers. People with these colours constantly dominant, never seem to sit still, and are impatient and often irritated when they can't travel.

LEMON YELLOW

POSITIVE TRAITS

This colour indicates vibrancy, general wellbeing and happiness. It often occurs during a successful phase, when the person is enjoying every aspect of life. The aura literally shines with positive energy, signalling that the person is going through a time of mental agility and rational thinking. Lemon yellow is seen in the auras of people with a strong sense of direction and those with the ability to be flexible and focus on many different aspects of their work at once.

NEGATIVE TRAITS

Lemon yellow can mean that the person is nervous about the future, feeling restless and uncertain of the events that are about to unfold. It also reveals a competitive spirit, but to the extent that the person might resort to deceit and manipulation to achieve their goals.

COMMON COMBINATIONS

Lemon yellow and orange

Although people with these two colours in their aura have a practical mind, they also tend to be dogmatic and highly critical of others. These people feel they must have some kind of recognition and may appear pompous and loud in company. They are jovial to the extreme and rely to a great extent on the company of others, rather than being happy alone.

Lemon yellow and sky blue

This combination is typical of people who have clarity of vision and are also intuitive and responsive to the world around them. They are spontaneous and enthusiastic, with a sunny disposition, yet there is an almost dreamy quality to the way they express themselves.

AMBER

POSITIVE TRAITS

The person who is consciously seeking change and development in their life often displays amber in their aura. It is the colour of strength and purpose and there is great originality and intelligence, happiness and playfulness. When amber is dominant, the person has the courage of their convictions and is convinced that they can win any argument or come through any conflict. It often appears in the aura when someone is in the process of applying for a new job – and has to make a good impression – or taking exams or tests.

NEGATIVE TRAITS

The only downside of amber is that people with it dominant in their aura can become too arrogant and assume that they will inspire everyone around them with their charisma. Often this colour is evident in the aura when people are convinced they can make someone happy, or that they can influence others to do things 'their way'.

COMMON COMBINATIONS

Amber and light green

With these two colours, there is an ability to succeed and a sense of joy, coupled with a strong original or eccentric streak. Amber and light green are found in the auras of people who are enjoying their work and aren't too serious about the future. They are relaxed, just taking life as it comes, but ready for any surprises or new opportunities.

Amber and red

This combination fuses passion and willpower with originality and determination to succeed. People with these colours dominant in their aura are usually pushing their way to the top of their profession, or are in the hot seat making important decisions or discovering new territory.

ORANGE

POSITIVE TRAITS

Joy, friendship and good times are all associated with orange. It represents opportunity, social interaction and the ability to really enjoy living. It is the colour of success and motivation, and usually denotes an extrovert personality or someone who likes to be in the public eye. Orange is often in the aura when a person is full of vitality and energy. The colour indicates a healthy attitude towards other people, there are no power agendas here, yet if it is dominant in the aura for long periods the person usually becomes successful in the public arena. When orange occurs in short bursts in the aura it indicates someone who is vibrant and witty, ready to talk to anyone and genuinely interested in them. Orange means someone has the ability to communicate and share their thoughts without a care in the world.

NEGATIVE TRAITS

The person may be so enthusiastic about everyone else – friends or colleagues – that they forget about their own needs and values. This can lead to mental and physical exhaustion, as well as disconnection from emotions and feelings.

COMMON COMBINATIONS

Orange and red
These two colours often appear in the auras of those who are fiercely self-willed but have not made it to the top of their profession or career. When people are frustrated in their efforts to achieve something – whether a promotion or simply running to catch the bus and missing it – orange and red often occur for short periods of time.

Orange and lavender
This combination indicates a need for peace, joy and tranquillity, although such people are still vibrant and lively – they simply need to recharge their batteries. It often occurs when people are about to take a holiday and still have office politics on their mind, or a sense of being indispensable, when in fact the office can get on quite well without them.

COPPER

POSITIVE TRAITS

This colour is associated with the Earth, with a feeling of being rooted and practical in all aspects of life. There is an enthusiasm for mundane projects at work, combined with a pragmatic and hard-working nature. People who are restoring or redecorating their homes, changing their gardens or involved in craft projects often have some copper in their aura; those with copper dominant are often involved in professions where self-discipline and dedication are prerequisites for success. Common sense and a tendency to follow convention are also often associated with this colour.

NEGATIVE TRAITS

Copper sometimes appears in the auras of people who don't feel motivated to make any changes in their life or improve their situation — it often occurs in those with sedentary jobs. They have slowed to a halt and don't want to be inspired or fired with enthusiasm. They feel that life is dull and nothing ever happens to them.

COMMON COMBINATIONS

Copper and yellow

This is a good combination for optimism and tact. It denotes people who are able to display enthusiasm and motivation, but are also always ready to listen and take care to be discreet. This combination often occurs in the auras of diplomats, lawyers and people who work in PR.

Copper and dark blue

People who have discovered that they need to take a new direction in life and are content to take things slowly often have copper and dark blue in their aura. They are honest, have an ethical approach to work and can be relied on and trusted in a crisis. The combination frequently occurs in the aura when people are making important decisions or re-evaluating their objectives.

PINK

POSITIVE TRAITS

Various shades of pink occur in the aura, but generally it is an indicator that warm-heartedness, love, harmony and a sense of vocation are present. Large areas of pink in a person's aura are a sign that they are in the throes of a passionate relationship, and red usually occurs as well. If the pink is almost iridescent, or loud and sharp, this indicates lust and sexual desire. Many young people have this as a blaze of colour in their aura when they first fall in love. Sometimes pink appears when someone is feeling loving towards their friends, children or parents. This is more likely to be a warmer pink, with a hint of orange-yellow. Very pale pink, with bluish undertones, implies infatuation; salmon pink suggests the person is in tune with their true vocation.

NEGATIVE TRAITS

A dusty, dirty pink indicates that the person is fooling around and being irresponsible about their feelings. There is no genuine love of anything, and this suggests an immature attitude.

COMMON COMBINATIONS

Pink and dark green
People who have pink and dark green together in their aura have a caring temperament and empathy with those in trouble or who are less fortunate than they are. The colours often occur when people are ambitious to succeed and take great pleasure in all aspects of their job, from the work itself to their interactions with colleagues.

Pink and white
This combination occurs in people who are strongly spiritual, or who are about to find themselves at a new and harmonious point in their life. It indicates people who are daydreamers or who need to attend to the spiritual side of their nature. It often appears in the auras of those who long to be in love.

LIGHT RED

POSITIVE TRAITS

Joy, sexuality and femininity are always associated with light red. When it is dominant in the aura, this suggests the person is involved in a relationship that is erotic
and deeply sexual. There is always a quality of mystery and glamour when this
colour is vibrant, so it is often seen in the auras of charismatic men and women
who radiate sexual desire and have magnetic personalities. It is not as impulsive
and as dynamic as the other reds, but gentle, sensitive and almost serene. People
with this colour permanently in their aura are not afraid to express themselves
through their sexual or sensual side.

NEGATIVE TRAITS

This colour can indicate that the person has an excessive desire for sexual
contact or the need to prove that they are very sexy. It also occurs in people who
are insecure about their sexuality or are always looking at themselves in the
mirror, unsure of their identity. (Often it shows in the auras of younger people,
particularly when they are preparing to go out on their first date.)

COMMON COMBINATIONS

Light red and orange
With their wonderful blend of enthusiasm for living and natural charisma, people
with light red and orange in their aura are both sexual and warm. This combination may occur when someone is involved in a deeply committed relationship;
alternatively, it appears in the auras of professionals who know how to make the
best of their sexual vitality and other talents.

Light red and sky blue
This combination shows an ability to be both imaginative and aware of the needs
of others. There is great sensitivity and caring, coupled with a light-hearted love
of life. These people are able to enjoy themselves alone and do not have to rely
on others for a sense of wellbeing.

SCARLET

POSITIVE TRAITS

The intensity of scarlet reflects a powerful ego and a strong will. It is the colour of passion and desire, as well as reflecting progress and achievement. Older people who have this colour dominant in their aura are sure of their own direction and purpose. Scarlet reflects an ability to attune easily to ideas and future plans, and can signify a time when a person's greatest fantasies and dreams can benefit their creative work.

NEGATIVE TRAITS

When it occurs in the auras of younger people, scarlet may indicate anger or aggression. It can mark a time when the person needs to assert their views or argue their case. Scarlet appears in the aura when people are nervous, impatient or over-anxious.

COMMON COMBINATIONS

Scarlet and crimson

When scarlet is fused with crimson in the aura, it signifies that the person may have recently been drawn into a new and passionate relationship. It can also indicate envy or jealousy.

Scarlet and yellow

This combination appears when a person is deceiving themselves about a partner's real motives, or when someone they thought they could trust is betraying them. It often occurs when there is disharmony between what people desire and the reality of the situation. It can also signify great loneliness, the passion for life depleted by excessive thinking.

Scarlet and dark blue

An intuitive ability, though not always consciously recognised, is associated with these two colours. They are evident in people who have a tendency to be dramatic about everything, perhaps even exaggerating the situation. They may feel fortunate and insightful, experiencing a flash of inspiration about events – often saying 'I knew I was right'.

CLARET

POSITIVE TRAITS

This deep colour often appears when a person is making a career change or trying to discover their direction. An abundance of claret reflects dynamic enthusiasm and the need to be noticed or somehow make oneself known in the world. It can also signify deep feelings and wishful thinking.

NEGATIVE TRAITS

The person may feel quick-tempered and impulsive, with an urge to take responsibility for everyone else around them. It may also be a testing time for making decisions and resolving a difficult crisis. People who have this colour dominant in their aura are often encountering difficulties with their feelings and can become overbearing and demanding.

COMMON COMBINATIONS

Claret and light blue

This combination appears in people who are feeling insecure inside, but who outwardly display an abundance of self-confidence. They may be unable to make decisions for themselves, but find it easy to take responsibility for everyone else. Others may find these people offer a ready shoulder to cry on and often turn to them for sorting out personal problems.

Claret and royal blue

People who know where they are going in life often have claret and royal blue together in their aura. Such people are full of commitment, with unshakable honesty and judgement. A sense of vocation is important to them at this time, or they may be ready to take on a more demanding role at work.

Claret and fuchsia pink

This vibrant combination is associated with falling in love. People may be buzzing with happiness and overwhelmed by deeper feelings. They might even be obsessed with someone who doesn't even know them – this is powerful energy so use it wisely.

INTERPRETING AURAS

The colours seen via the aura-imaging camera depend on the subject's mood and personality and the balance of mind, body and spirit at the time the image is captured. The camera captures the essence of the moment by translating electromagnetic impulses from the hands, which rest on plates placed on either side of the person as they sit in front of the lens. When the camera is operated, it combines the hands' electrical impulses with a photograph, usually of the head and shoulders, and shows the aura as visible colours on a Polaroid. On the following pages are some real-life examples to show you how you can interpret the patterns of colours in a person's aura.

name: Alex **age:** 48
occupation: cabin crew
at Gatwick airport
The dominant violet and turquoise colours of Alex's aura indicate he lives in the world of imagination and dreams. He currently prefers to talk about dreams and miracles – even winning the lottery – rather than the mundane practicalities of life. He feels safer in his imagination, and could well be developing his psychic abilities. He needs a peaceful and quiet period to recharge his physical batteries. Often when people have high levels of these colours dominant in their aura it also means they need to develop a better awareness of their spiritual nature. He requires plenty of time for relaxation, reflection and contemplation to come to terms with his emotional nature.

name: Dan **age:** 24

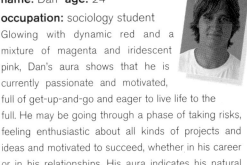

occupation: sociology student
Glowing with dynamic red and a mixture of magenta and iridescent pink, Dan's aura shows that he is currently passionate and motivated, full of get-up-and-go and eager to live life to the full. He may be going through a phase of taking risks, feeling enthusiastic about all kinds of projects and ideas and motivated to succeed, whether in his career or in his relationships. His aura indicates his natural ability to be in the right place at the right time. Basically, he's lucky at the moment. His aura reveals a creative and charismatic personality, a powerful sexual drive and strong ego, and the will to succeed. He is assertive and sometimes has impulsive urges to make decisions quickly.

name: Rebecca **age:** 25
occupation: junior editor
There's a wonderful feeling of creative ideas, intuition and passionate desire in Rebecca's aura. She has a well-balanced combination of colours – dark red reveals her lively and passionate approach to life, while the soft pink reveals her warm nature. Notice an area of pink close to her heart, implying that she is currently in love, or at least in the mood for it. The range of light blues and greens indicate she is feeling inspired and has a clear view of where she is going in life, although she would rather avoid the practical aspects and does not want to concern herself with the boring daily routines. At the moment, Rebecca is probably feeling very creative and sensitive to the world around her – this is not the aura of a pragmatist, but someone who is full of imagination.

name: Clare **age:** 37

occupation: designer

With so much white in her aura, Clare would do well to develop her intuitive and psychic skills, if she has not already connected to them. She may have a very chameleon-like personality at the moment, able to adapt to any situation. This huge splash of white may indicate that she is going through a major change in her life. The change is necessary – and will have a positive outcome – but because it is depleting her energy levels, she may need to start doing more physical exercise or work on balancing her mind, body and spirit to get vitalized again. The violets and purplish blues in Clare's aura reveal she can create a magical environment around her. She has strong insight and could almost be telepathic if she knew how to channel such energy. At the moment she may prefer to live in her imagination, with dreams being very important.

name: Owen **age:** 18

occupation: art student

Owen's aura reveals his bubbly, outgoing personality and his ability to communicate and get on with anyone, in any situation. He's fun-loving and charming, with a great sense of humour, and his social life is of the utmost importance to him now. The strong orange presence in Owen's aura suggests he is creative with words and that he can concentrate for long stretches. This colour often shows up in writers and salespeople. The softer orange suggests he's studying hard to make his career work for him and that he's self-controlled and disciplined when he needs to be. The softer green and violet indicate that for all his fun-loving, cheeky nature, he is sensitive and compassionate and is a practical idealist – he can use his imagination and ground it in reality.

name: Amy **age:** 22

occupation: MA student

in theatre direction

This aura is positively brimming with friendliness and determination to succeed. The greens on the right of the picture suggest that Amy is reliable and open-minded, that she has great belief in her career and is adaptable and willing to try anything once. The strong sage greens, in particular, suggest she has the dedication to advance and reach whatever goals she has set for herself. The softer turquoise colours indicate she is idealistic about her relationships, but is currently happy with the way things are. She is supportive of her friends and colleagues, indicated by the area of apricot. The fact that this colour turns to pink suggests she is currently in love or thinking about love.

name: Kate **age:** 36

occupation: nurse/mother

Although this aura displays a cloud of white, the intensity of the blue around the edge and the strong presence of greeny grey and violet outweigh the density of whiteness. The greeny-grey suggests Kate is currently going through a period when making decisions about her future could be proving difficult, particularly regarding her relationships. The splash of violet also indicates she may have begun to work on the spiritual aspects of her life and develop an awareness of her imaginative world. With so much deep blue surrounding her aura, she is sensitive to the needs of others and wants to communicate her feelings. She may feel that the moral issues in her life need attention, and there seems to be a great weight on her shoulders, as if she is unable to progress on her chosen path until certain responsibilities have been resolved.

71

name: Gary **age:** 43

occupation: hotelier

The deep rich blue and the blend of greens and yellows suggest a deep integrity and someone who knows they have chosen the right direction in life. Gary is both compassionate and steadfast in his feelings and loyalties, but he takes a long time to trust anyone. There is an unusual amount of olive green in his aura, which can indicate a suspicion of the motives of others. In his career he can be totally reliable, but he often has his own reasons for making decisions others wouldn't dare take, simply because he must prove himself right at all costs. He's very stubborn when it comes to making changes in his own personal environment, although he likes to see others changing theirs. Being awkward for the sake of being awkward is sometimes a common trait with this balance of colours in the aura.

name: Josie **age:** 12

occupation: schoolchild

This is a tranquil yet powerful aura. The area of pale green and the quality of all the colours denote a strong personality and someone who has great purpose in life. There is very little cloudiness, indicating someone who is attuned to the natural world and has a sense of the divine in all things. Josie's aura reveals that she is intuitive and has a high level of mental achievement. Using her intuitive sense to help her make decisions means she can take advantage of opportunities that come along now. The clarity of the aura also indicates clear-sightedness. She is practical and yet sensitive enough to be able to use her resources towards creating a better future for herself. She has a harmonious nature and the number of clear blues suggests she can communicate successfully and understand other people and their needs.

name: Darren **age:** 31

occupation: marketing and promotions manager

There is a wonderful mix of greens and blues in this aura, with a dash of aquamarine. Darren seems well balanced and currently has a harmonious life, but there is a certain coolness and aloofness about his aura. The aquamarine colours suggest he needs a considerable amount of freedom and space at the moment, and he's not interested in forming a deeply intimate relationship with anyone. He simply needs to have more fun. He's sensitive yet practical, so won't take too many risks in his career, preferring instead to concentrate on the work in hand. He is compassionate and caring towards his friends and colleagues, but has a vulnerable side and probably feels more secure if he keeps his relationships with others detached and airy, rather than close and emotional.

name: Terry **age:** 61

occupation: actor

The symmetry of Terry's aura is a sign of a hard-working and dedicated personality. He may be unable to connect to his intuitive side at the moment, but there is a strong likelihood that he could develop his psychic or telepathic abilities if he wanted to. He's acutely sensitive, but probably won't admit it. The strong emphasis on blues and aquamarines denotes someone who loves to communicate and also requires plenty of freedom to do as he chooses. He currently needs to relax and devote more time to peace and tranquillity. This even flow of colours often suggests someone who is happiest when out on the wide open sea, fishing or simply whiling away the time in a boat.

name: Caroline **age:** 44

occupation: movement teacher/visual and performing artist

There's a slightly cloudy feeling to the violet area around Caroline's face and an interesting splash of white around her throat. She is currently very sensitive and needs to take time to relax and enjoy a tranquil lifestyle. The turquoise areas suggest she is trying to find out what she truly values in life. The violet colours around her face indicate her imagination is powerful, she's in harmony with her ideals, but she may find it hard to be rational and make difficult decisions. The white around her throat shows she may be having problems communicating her needs in a relationship, or that she needs to develop her own voice. There is a gentleness about the aura that indicates she is deeply reflective.

name: Wilf **age:** 9

occupation: schoolchild

The auras of young people are always fascinating simply because they are so unclouded by adult responsibilities and psychological complexes. Wilf has a vibrant, exciting and dynamic aura. The oranges, reds and yellows indicate he's brimming with nervous energy and a sense of get-up-and-go. He's motivated and enthusiastic and probably gets bored easily. Hyperactivity is often common with these colours; Wilf's need for variety and plenty of entertainment is essential for him now. The orange-yellow dominance also indicates a powerful mind. The area of light blue reflects his struggle towards maturity, and is often seen in young people who need to develop their artistic skills. The small pink area around his heart chakra shows how loving and gentle he is under the extrovert personality.

name: Sharon **age:** 43

occupation: mother

This aura is very difficult to interpret, simply because it is clouded by current doubts and fears. It may also be that when the photo was taken Sharon was nervous about the outcome. The clouds that almost obscure most of the head may indicate she does not want to see the truth about herself, or that she is blinding herself to something in her life that needs evaluation or clear thinking. The pink to violet hues around the edge suggest she loves living in the world of her imagination, is creative and needs to be in a tender and warm relationship. If she is fearful of the result of the photograph, this may mean that there are certain aspects of her life that need attention. Is it her relationships, or is she not sure of her career or the direction her life is taking?

name: Paul **age:** 38

occupation: creative director for music collective

With its clear and expressive colours, Paul's aura denotes a harmonious attitude to life and a fairly easygoing and warm personality. The pink area suggests he's currently involved in a loving and caring relationship, but because it is connected to the green areas of his aura it also indicates he has a true sense of vocation — he loves his work. The soft blues and deeper blues all suggest a creative and inspired mind; he possibly works hard to develop original thinking or new ideas for future projects. The clarity of the colours shows he's motivated, but not ruthless. Generally, Paul is healthy and energetic, and his aura reveals a personality that is able to cope with any crisis. He's a smooth operator, but has enough insight and clarity of vision to ensure he doesn't become arrogant, vain or egotistical.

name: Mari **age:** 39

occupation: editor

This is the aura of a practical idealist. Mari is capable of implementing ideas and, using her insight and common sense, dealing with any situation. The large areas of green indicate she is motivated and ambitious, although she may currently be unsure of which direction to take, suggested by the cloudiness of the aura over her head. The aquamarine hues are a sign that fun and social interaction are vital for her wellbeing now. Freedom to make her own decisions is essential, otherwise she can feel trapped. Although she is sensitive to other people's feelings and moods, she feels she has to make a big impression to succeed, when in fact her calm, unflappable manner and genuine compassion are the secrets of her popularity and progress. The small pink area on her chest indicates that she is currently in love or has deeply warm feelings for someone special.

name: Hazel **age:** 52

occupation: mature student in public policy and administration/mother

The clarity of Hazel's aura indicates that she has a balanced approach to life at the moment. The almost pumpkin-orange area shows she has self-restraint and can control most situations easily. In fact, she also needs to feel in control and won't be happy unless she knows exactly what's going on in her environment. She needs to develop her extrovert nature and not to worry about what others think of her. Her organisational and practical skills are revealed by the green hues, but with so much blue also in evidence she may be acutely sensitive to other people's moods and feelings and unable to access her own values and needs. She is motivated and has firm goals, but it's likely that she's too often swayed by the ideas and opinions of others, rather than listening to her own inner voice.

name: Stuart **age:** 27

occupation: journalist

Vitality and lust for life are evident in Stuart's aura. The strong middle red area denotes passion for everything he does and an impulsive and often impetuous side to his nature. He likes to move fast and take risks. He doesn't have time to worry about what happened yesterday, tomorrow is always more inspiring and important. The various shades of orange indicate an extrovert personality and the ability to mix with anyone. He's ambitious and could be ruthless about his career progress, needing to set goals for himself constantly. What other people say to him rarely matters, but he's devoted to his friends and passionate about those he truly cares for. The touch of pale blue in his aura, and the softer pink around his chest area, suggest there is hidden vulnerability and a creative side to his nature. He is sensitive, but won't let it show, so is melodramatic instead.

name: Dave **age:** 61

occupation: commodities trader

Although it contains a common combination of colours, Dave's aura is splashed with a wash of whites and light hues from both the greens and blues of the spectrum. He is focused and clear about his current needs and ambitions, but prefers to ignore the underlying motivations for why he is making particular choices right now. He needs to relax and enjoy himself, to form a sense of self-development and really get to know his spiritual and imaginative side. He may already have embarked upon an inner journey, but he needs to feel a connection to the energy within, rather than just thinking about it. His imagination and sensitivity are powerful – he genuinely cares about others and enjoys being in good company. The more mundane daily routines of his current lifestyle probably mean he can't be as compassionate as he would like to be.

THE VERDICT

Alex

Dreaming and escaping to a world of the imagination are ways in which I seek refuge from the stress of modern life. The reference to my needing to develop my spiritual nature is perhaps recognition of the fact that I am a sceptic.

Amy

The analysis shows a clear emphasis on the importance of my career, which is the focal point of my life at present. When it comes to relationships, I am a realist, which is probably why I'm currently single.

Dan

Pretty much spot on. The suggestion that I have the ability to be in the right place at the right time is especially true; I often land on my feet. I'm not so sure that I am particularly assertive, though.

Kate

Interesting. It was not difficult for me to relate to this description. I am very secure in my relationships. As a nurse, I do consider that I am caring.

Rebecca

Although I'm still sceptical, I have to admit that I thought my analysis pretty accurate. I am positive about the direction my life is taking, and I feel that my level of creativity is running high, with lots of ideas waiting to be put into action.

Gary

I am stunned by the accuracy of the analysis. It tells all about the way I am. I am very impressed!

Josie

I didn't know anything about auras before having my photo taken, but now I think it's all fascinating. It is amazing how much can be interpreted from them!

Clare

I really enjoyed this reading and I can recognize myself here. I shall be following the advice to take physical exercise to combat low energy. Perhaps next time I have my aura photographed it'll be a bit more perky!

Darren

I thought this quite accurate; it described my current emotional state very well. Boys just want to have fun! Overall I was very impressed with the whole event, and I'd recommend it to anyone with an interest in this sort of thing.

Owen

It is reassuring to know that as a practical idealist with the ability to study hard I am heading towards a promising career, and encouraging to know that I am likely to enjoy a lively social life.

Terry

They say the truth hurts, and in case of my aura reading it certainly does smart. A wonderfully exact and true reading.

Caroline

An accurate picture I think, especially regarding communication in a relationship. The 'difficulty' of a possible decision, and time for fruitful introspection: these points added to things I have been reflecting upon lately. But I don't consider myself irrational.

Wilf

Wilf's mum Kate says: 'Wilf is a typical nine-year-old, full of energy. Perhaps being a middle child he doesn't get the attention he'd like. He does love drawing detailed pictures.'

Sharon

I was surprised at my analysis. I was not at all nervous about the outcome; I was confident and happy. I am in a tender and warm relationship, and at my age I think I do know the truth about myself. I am not at all like the person described.

Paul

Pretty accurate. It describes my state of mind and way of working well, and hits the nail on the head in my feelings about my partner and my career. A revealing and thought-provoking experience!

Mari

I wouldn't mind being the person described; that's the key to the success of the analysis, I imagine. And that person also felt more familiar to me than any of the other analyses. I admit, I'm intrigued. I showed the reading to the person responsible for the pink spot over my heart, and he said, 'Sweet.'

Hazel

Until recently this was a new area for me. I approached it with an open mind, rather like an explorer. I can see a plausible link between feeling and colour, which can be read and interpreted. What's interesting is that each reading is different, and unique.

Stuart

Though many of my true charac-teristics – personal and public – were correctly pinpointed, there were enough basic flaws to highlight the method's 'touch and go' success rate. Anyone who knows me will tell you that I'm the least melodramatic person they know.

Dave

I am pleasantly surprised at the generally accurate findings. It is true that I have not yet fully exploited my potential. And the alarmingly correct deduction was made that I need to relax and enjoy life more. There was also a correct finding that I'm imaginative and sensitive. By and large, an accurate and good reading.

CHAPTER FOUR

AURA COLOURS AND THE OTHER SENSES

If you have worked on developing all your senses, as outlined in Chapter 2, you don't have to rely on being able to see the aura physically or look at an aura-imaging photograph. You can now begin to interpret the other senses to discover which of the ten basic colours is currently the most vivid in your aura or those of your friends. To do this, you will need to look at the ten different keywords for each sense: hearing (pages 82–83), touch (pages 84–85), smell (pages 86–87) and intuition (pages 88–89).

You can use all your senses to 'see' the colours in
an aura, not just your sense of sight.

READING OTHER PEOPLE'S AURAS

Use the sense you feel happiest with first. For example, if you have found it easy to hear different qualities in the sounds of people's voices or in music then use the sound keywords in order to interpret a friend's aura.

Read through the brief descriptions of each keyword and choose the one that seems to correspond most closely to what you are sensing from your friend, whether you're using your sense of smell, touch, hearing or intuition. Then look at the chart on page 91. This tells you which of the ten different sounds corresponds to which colour, or which of the ten different smells corresponds to which colour, and so on.

If you decide to use more than one sense to determine the predominant colour in the aura – for example, if there isn't much difference between two senses with which you feel comfortable – you may find more than one colour is powerful in your friend's aura. This is normal. You will notice from the sample aura interpretations (pages 68–77) that combinations of several colours appear in the aura more often than a single colour.

When you first start reading auras, however, it is important to get to know the basic principles first, so the colour you first discovered using your favourite sense is currently the most powerful colour in the aura. The second colour can of course also be taken into account. Once you get used to combining colour readings you will find you begin to read several colours together without having to look at them separately.

When you have matched the type of sound, smell, touch or intuition you sensed to a basic colour according to the aura colour checklist chart, read the appropriate colour profiles (pages 92–101) to find out your friend's current auric state and how they can benefit from the knowledge. You can also read about the colours in Chapter 3 (pages 48–67).

HOW TO FIND YOUR OWN CURRENT AURIC COLOUR

You can't exactly sit and listen to your own voice or smell your own aroma. So, in order to check out which main auric colour you are expressing at the moment, use the same keywords but in a different way.

On a piece of paper, write down the keyword list for each sense and give a maximum score of 10 to the quality of the sense you like most, 9 to the next, and so on down to 1 for the one you like least or are indifferent to. For example, from the sound keywords (page 83) you may prefer sexy voices above them all, so score 10; followed by vibrant ones second, so score 9; right down through the rest of the words until you reach deep voices, to which you may be indifferent – so score 1. Score all four senses in the same way. Then add up the scores for each colour by using the chart on page 91.

Don't forget, as your moods, feelings and circumstances change so does your aura, so do the test at regular intervals to see if your response to the keywords changes.

INTERPRETING SOUNDS

For each of the ten sound keywords below read the brief description of their essential qualities and how they apply to people. Then look at the box on the opposite page to help you work out your friend's aura colour or your own.

DEEP voices make you feel calm and sometimes very down to earth with their deep bass, which often has a gravelly quality. People with deep voices sound practical, pragmatic or quietly ambitious.

PURRING voices have the calming, relaxing effect of a cat's purr, sounding as if they could stroke you with rhythmical words. Someone with a voice like that sounds serene and unworldly.

RIPPLING voices convey the sound of waves swashing across a shingle beach or of fingers trailing to and fro in water. People with rippling voices sound as if they are sure of what they want to say, and whatever they say seems to be perfectly phrased.

SEXY voices are exactly that – unmistakably rich and sensual. People with sexy tones sound passionate and erotic. There is a truly magnetic and sexual quality to their voice, and their words are languorous, musical and meaningful.

SILKY voices are gentle, flowing and compassionate. There is both affection and wisdom behind the words. People with silky voices sound as if they are willing to listen to and encourage others.

SILVERY voices are beautifully pitched and harmonious, adding a musical quality to speech. People with such voices talk quietly and slowly, serious about what they are saying; they rarely make a fuss, become angry or lose control.

SOFT voices make you feel warm and loved, with their quality of empathy and tenderness. Those with soft voices sound as if they are truly concerned about the world – and you – as they use well-meaning and carefully chosen words.

TUNEFUL voices are playful, curious and melodious, conveying a sense of honesty, joy and a love of communicating. People with tuneful voices sound as if they are excited about life and adore exploring all kinds of ideas.

VELVETY voices make you feel as if you are being wrapped in this sumptuous cloth. There is a sensuous quality to these voices, but it is sensitive and clear, not provocative or sexual. People with velvety voices sound as if they have great imagination and insight – every word is spoken with meaning.

VIBRANT voices are lively, sibilant, buzzy and fun to listen to. People with such voices convey enthusiasm – they exude happiness through what they say and there is often a crescendo of words followed by laughter.

Depending on your mood, you may prefer the vibrant, deep notes of a CD to the silvery, soft sounds of water.

SOUND KEYWORDS

Deep

Purring

Rippling

Sexy

Silky

Silvery

Soft

Tuneful

Velvety

Vibrant

FOR YOUR FRIEND

To find out your friend's aura colour using your hearing, sit quietly chatting together and concentrate on what their voice sounds like. From the list above, choose the word that best describes it. Then turn to the chart on page 91 to find the corresponding colour.

FOR YOURSELF

Rate the above sounds on a scale of 10 to 1 according to your current preferences. Score 10 for the sound you like the most, down to 1 for the one you like least or to which you are indifferent. Do the same for the other sense keywords and then add up your scores for each colour by using the chart on page 91.

INTERPRETING TOUCH

Touching someone's aura can feel as prickly as a thistle or as smooth as a baby's cheek.

For each of the ten touch keywords below read the brief description of their essential qualities and how they apply to people. Then look at the box on the opposite page to help you work out your friend's aura colour or your own. With these interpretations, remember that when you touch an aura you are in fact touching the energy of that person.

COOL to the touch. This feels like refreshing water. There is a sense of calmness and stillness about these people, who seem unflappable and unhurried. Those who exude cool energy communicate well and convey a feeling of profound understanding.

EVEN to the touch. This feels unblemished, sleek and unruffled. People who exude even energy convey a sense of stillness and the ability to heal others. There is also a sense of magical enchantment and the need for everything to be in harmony around them.

HOT to the touch. This feels powerful – heat radiates from these people and there is a sense of dynamic or passionate energy. Those who exude hot energy also convey a feeling of challenge and action. They have strong emotions and a great love of life.

POLISHED to the touch. This feels slippery, glossy, glazed, glassy or buttery. There is a sense of suave gentility, tranquillity and relaxation. People who exude polished energy convey a

sense of self-awareness and positive thinking, they are kind and practical idealists.

PRICKLY to the touch. This feels sharp, spiky and often serrated. There is a sense of carelessness, as well as vibrancy and wellbeing. People who exude prickly energy are often motivated and successful, extrovert and undaunted by what the future may hold.

ROUGH to the touch. This feels uneven, bumpy, jagged and unpredictable. There is a sense of agility, flexibility and restlessness. People who exude rough aura convey a feeling of boundless energy, excitability and tremendous vitality.

SMOOTH to the touch. This feels like satin or silk, the energy is sleek and soothing. There is a sense of sensitivity and purpose. People who exude smooth energy convey a feeling of deliberation and common sense; they are conscious of the power of their imagination and are able to use it with ingenuity.

TEXTURED to the touch. This feels granular and organic. There is a sense of woven form and the energy is structured and organized. People who exude textured energy appear to be shrewdly confident – they are frequently unflappable and down to earth.

UNDULATING to the touch. This feels pulsating, rolling and rhythmical, attuned to the cycles of the solar system. People who exude undulating energy seem to have complete faith in and devotion to their purpose. There is a feeling of psychic awareness.

WARM to the touch. This feels like magical energy, with the warmth radiating from these people in the most loving and caring way. Those who exude warm energy convey a feeling of commitment and a genuine love of others.

TOUCH KEYWORDS

Cool

Even

Hot

Polished

Prickly

Rough

Smooth

Textured

Undulating

Warm

FOR YOUR FRIEND

To find out your friend's aura colour using touch, you need to do some of the sense development exercises in Chapter 2. Try to touch your friend's auric field, before an auric embrace or massage. From the list above, choose a word to describe what your friend's aura feels like to touch. Then turn to the chart on page 91 to find the corresponding colour.

FOR YOURSELF

Rate the above words on a scale of 10 to 1 according to the type of energy you like to touch in other people's auras. Score 10 for the one you like the most, 1 for the one you like least. Do the same for the other sense keywords and then add up your scores for each colour by using the chart on page 91.

INTERPRETING SMELLS

For each of the ten smell keywords below read the brief description of their essential qualities and how they apply to people. Then look at the box on the opposite page to help you work out your friend's aura colour or your own.

BALMY smells are almost undetectable. They are essences, rather than strong aromas, and include the fragile scents of lemon balm and other oil-rich plants such as olives, sunflowers and coconuts. These people convey a sense of magic, as if they know many secrets and are spiritually wise.

EARTHY smells include aromas like coffee beans in a percolator, newly mown lawns and fresh potting compost. They apply to people who wear little perfume and prefer their own natural fragrance. There is often a hint of autumn leaves in these people's aroma, and they convey a sense of ambition and gentle strength.

FRESH smells include the salty smell when you've been in the sea, the smell of earth when the sun comes out after a downpour, and the smell of morning dew. Sea minerals, mineral water and spas are all the kinds of aroma that are associated with freshness. People with a fresh aroma convey a sense of peaceful sensitivity.

HERBAL smells include the fragrances of rosemary, sage, thyme, parsley and lavender. There's a sweetness mixed with an almost spicy pungent quality. These people smell as if they have just walked in from a field of lavender; they convey a sense of light-heartedness and spontaneity.

MUSKY smells include perfumes with a high degree of musk, civet, ambergris and sandalwood. People often wear these scents to enhance their own, creating a sexy, erotic impression. Their skin may have a musky aroma when they've been sunbathing or perspiring.

SMOKY smells include those of cigarettes, autumn bonfires and burned toast; they express a truthful and intuitive quality. People who smell smoky aren't necessarily smokers. Non-smokers generally do not have a particularly strong smell about them, they just seem quietly aromatic, as if they had been sitting warming their hands over a log fire for a while.

PIQUANT smells include those of chutneys, pickles and vinegar, as well as peppery aromas like highly seasoned sauces, spring onions and garlic. People who smell piquant convey a positive attitude that is compassionate and practical.

Above right: There's a world of difference between the smell of a fragrant rose and cigarettes, but other smells may be harder to distinguish, so you need to train your nose.

SMELL KEYWORDS

Balmy

Earthy

Fresh

Herbal

Musky

Smoky

Piquant

Spicy

Sweet

Tangy

FOR YOUR FRIEND

When trying to find out your friend's aura colour by smell, your first impression is the most important. Ask your friend to go for a brief walk in the fresh air then to come back inside. From the list above, choose a word to describe the aroma or fragrance your friend conveys as they enter the room. Then turn to the chart on page 91 to find the corresponding colour.

FOR YOURSELF

Rate the above words on a scale of 10 to 1 according to the aromas you currently like. Score 10 for the smell you like the most, down to 1 for the one you like least. Do the same for the other sense keywords and then add up your scores for each colour by using the chart on page 91.

SPICY smells include perfumes with a lot of ginger, nutmeg or mace. Indian restaurants are renowned for their spicy smell. People often have a spicy aroma when they are excited about a new job or about to embark on an adventure or holiday. They convey a sense of enthusiasm and self-confidence.

SWEET smells include sugary or flowery perfumes, which people often unconsciously wear to emphasize their auric vibration. Some people, without wearing perfume, seem to exude a fragrance of sweet peas, honey or marzipan and convey a sense of warmth and happiness. Their personal aroma is somehow as fragile as rose petals or as sugary as strawberry jam.

TANGY smells include scents with a high degree of lemon, orange or clove. People often have a minty or zesty aroma about them when they're really nervous or have been rushing home from the office. Other tangy fragrances, which convey a lively extrovert quality, are limes, apples and grapefruit.

VIOLET

YOU NOW You are currently infused with psychic awareness. Violet radiates from those with spiritual strength and clairvoyant wisdom, so you may be going through a period when you can connect to your own spiritual purpose or belief.

FEELINGS You need to express yourself and will be naturally understanding of everyone else's sentiments. If you are not usually in touch with your feelings, try to listen to what they are telling you. It is a good time for self-development.

THOUGHTS You may want to communicate a general sense of wonder at the world and talk about miracles. Your thoughts may be peppered with fantasies and it is possible you may develop psychic connections with long-lost friends or relatives.

LIFESTYLE This is a time to reflect upon your life and where you are going. If you are interested in psychic or spiritual development, then you should start to work on your inner self. You may find you connect to new friends involved with alternative arts, such as astrology, t'ai chi or yoga, all beneficial to your future happiness.

CAREER Work may seem like the last place you want to be, but you'll be attuned to colleagues and their moods. Take the opportunity to relax and enjoy the ethereal magic of your imagination, so avoid making drastic changes, but ensure you maintain a deep sense of vocation. If violet remains a constant auric colour for you, you may find greater fulfilment working in the spiritual professions.

HEALTH Your energy levels are high and your awareness of your body's health superb. Relaxation techniques and a good diet are important, but you'll respond to your body's needs intuitively.

LAVENDER

YOU NOW Lavender is the colour that signifies being connected to a 'higher' energy. You are glowing with mystery and should take the chance to channel your healing power. Harmony, peace and quiet contemplation will be vital, so find time to enjoy your inner quest.

FEELINGS You feel radiant with unworldly magic, and you'll be compassionate and tolerant of all aspects of life. Healing energy means you can deal with any crisis or laugh with any friend. Your mere presence will teach others that you don't have to be emotional to have feelings.

THOUGHTS Your thinking at the moment is clear and pure. This is an excellent time for sorting out your problems, making precise plans or being inspired with ideas. Thoughts of harmony will also help others to sense your inner balance.

LIFESTYLE You're prepared to sit back and enjoy feeling in harmony and at one with the world. Rushing around in a frantic whirl and getting stressed won't be on your agenda. Everyday events have little meaning for you, but your mind, body and spirit are of the utmost importance.

CAREER At work, your presence – and even your voice on the phone – is a force that can heal others. Career changes won't be on your mind – you'd rather meditate on life and enjoy your leisure time or join in spiritual healing activities.

HEALTH Find plenty of time to relax and meditate or just go for long peaceful walks. Sleep will be filled with important dreams. Consider doing some dream-work (pages 40–41) to understand yourself better.

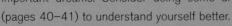

TURQUOISE

YOU NOW You are currently able to offer advice to friends and colleagues, and are feeling positive about life and your future. Radiating tranquillity and tolerance, you can encourage and nurture others with affection. Your relaxed and beneficial energy enlightens and gives inspiration to those around you.

FEELINGS You have deep and beautiful feelings about the world. Your positive attitude towards your own psychological growth is enhanced by your awareness of your emotions. The people you truly care for will benefit from your warm spirit and empathy now.

THOUGHTS Your thinking will be inspired, creative and visionary. The future will be more on your mind than the past, and plans and projects can be positively developed. This is a wonderful time for putting your ideas into action.

LIFESTYLE A relaxed social atmosphere will give you plenty of opportunity to indulge in peaceful, enjoyable harmony. Your polished and serene charisma means you'll want to be out and about, being the life and soul of the party and radiating joy. Now is the time to enjoy and liberate your refined yet practical sense of being.

CAREER Expressing your future plans is essential now. Look towards progress and making deliberate changes in your career. You can inspire the people who matter with your brilliant ideas and self-conviction, making a positive move towards improvement and achievement.

HEALTH This is a time for relaxation, peace and a short break from the rat race. With your high energy levels, however, you need physical exercise to channel your vitality, so you need to be balanced in your approach. Take a peaceful weekend off from routine, but don't equate it with doing nothing – try a workout or two and resolve to incorporate one into your daily life.

BLUE

YOU NOW This is a time when you are at your most harmonious and positive. You are experiencing a sense of profound inner peace and know exactly where you are going. You are sensitive to the needs of others, and although your feelings and moods may change daily, you have the determination and good judgement to succeed, whichever direction you choose to take.

FEELINGS You are calm and untroubled, able to express your emotions in a gentle and relaxed way. You don't get uptight or angry and are tolerant and understanding of other people and their moods and feelings.

THOUGHTS You have good hunches about what is happening and, in addition, your mind is focused and able to connect to these inner flashes of intuition. Although you are logical, you also hear your inner voice – your head does not rule your heart. Your thinking is clear and unmuddled and you enjoy making decisions then totally switching off to relax.

LIFESTYLE You need a restful time right now – perhaps consider taking a holiday or a short break from your normal routine. You're in the mood for experiencing tranquillity and the luxuries of life. Socially you will be at your most diplomatic and relaxed. You also feel fortunate and lucky.

CAREER You're ready to take on more responsibility. You are determined and feeling ready to progress, able to deal with all kinds of projects and develop important new strategies.

HEALTH Your energy levels are not as high as usual, although you feel relaxed, so it is important not to get stressed or mentally exhausted. Take time to meditate or simply rest. Conserve your energy for when you are next in a more dynamic mood. Do some simple stretching exercises and make small, positive changes in your diet.

AQUAMARINE

YOU NOW You are balanced and genuinely concerned about the happiness of your friends, loved ones and colleagues, although you may be going through a period of change in your own life. You are enterprising and caring, organised and sensible. People want to confide in you because you seem so rooted in reality. You feel supportive and capable, although you still need to feel a sense of freedom.

FEELINGS You fluctuate between intensely personal feelings and carefree moods. Sometimes you are profoundly vulnerable, at others noncommittal and untouched by the world around you. This means you are more responsive to other people and their feelings than your own, because your own can seem overwhelming or frustrating.

THOUGHTS With your clear, concise thinking, you enjoy mind games, exploring other people's problems and finding crazy solutions to the most impossible of problems. You have a strong mind and can use it to make important decisions and motivate others.

LIFESTYLE Making your social life lively and carefree and generally entertaining others is important to you now. Partners, family and friends come first, and you'll be surrounded by people who need your support and responsible attitude to getting things done. Find the time to indulge in your favourite form of relaxation, and don't let others make too many demands on you.

CAREER You are brimming with ideas and able to organise your creative thoughts and turn them into reality. You are in transition and will want to make important changes in your career while you are calm and relaxed. You have a feeling you'll be able to take on any new responsibility that comes your way.

HEALTH You are in excellent health and have achieved a level of fitness that won't go unnoticed. Build on this for the future in case you need to draw on your energy reserves later. As well as creating new goals, take the opportunity to pamper your body and your mind.

DEEP GREEN

YOU NOW You are working hard, you're ambitious and reliable and ready to make a success of your life. What is most important for you now is to make an excellent impression on others, whether friends, partners or colleagues. You feel the need to acquire prestige or achieve some kind of fame, and your will to achieve is powerful and committed. You are also down-to-earth and quietly enterprising.

FEELINGS You may not want to examine your feelings, preferring to make thoughts your aim, rather than revealing your emotions or moods. If external events trigger an emotional response, allow yourself to express your feelings and deal with them honestly, because at the moment you can face anything with integrity.

THOUGHTS Powerful thoughts are filling your mind and you're confident and certain about whatever you want to say. You'll be thinking about how you can improve your way of-life, or how you can make more money. Your thoughts are on the future rather than the past.

LIFESTYLE You are economical and careful with your finances because you are so practical and sensible right now. Social fun could offer you a chance to make valuable contacts or impress people that count. Your work and future will be more important than home and family, but you'll enjoy the company of friends and be ready to help out at a moment's notice if needed.

CAREER This is crucial for you now, and you'll be eager to make changes slowly to ensure you achieve the best possible success. You're motivated and

clear about your future and although you can be demanding, you'll also be generous and caring towards those who you can respect.

HEALTH Take a break and indulge in some gentle pampering – a leisurely massage, perhaps, or aromatherapy. Generally, detox your skin and take care of your body. Your energy levels are high, so keep yourself in tiptop shape while you have such vitality.

ORANGE

YOU NOW You are at your most original and independent. You can be as creative and enthusiastic as you like about any project, so now is the time to get on with all those things you've been wanting to do. You are ready to express your ideas and be at your most self-confident. You have a good rapport with people and a natural flair for saying the right thing at the right time. Luck is truly on your side at the moment.

FEELINGS You'll be feeling buzzy and high on your own creative dynamics. With this inspiration, you'll generate an atmosphere of enthusiasm and optimism wherever you go. You are full of humour and fun, so enjoy the experience of feeling really alive.

THOUGHTS You'll be thinking up all kinds of new brainwaves, schemes and projects. In fact, you'll have so many new ideas on your mind that you won't know which one to put into practice first. Your thoughts will be on having fun, so go out and inspire others with your wit and vibrant communicative skills.

LIFESTYLE Friends, socialising and generally getting out and about are essential for you now. Work and leisure will be of equal importance and you'll be genuinely fascinated by everyone you meet. You radiate happiness and joy, finding it easy to have a laugh and be the centre of attention.

CAREER You are ambitious, motivated and original; your ideas will put you in line for future promotion or better prospects. If you really want to succeed now your insight and creative talents won't go unnoticed.

HEALTH Don't let your enthusiasm make you forget to relax. You can be so absorbed in your creative urge that you don't think about your body's health. Although your mind and spirit are balanced and energised at the moment, you need to remember to spend some time alone to recharge those vibrant batteries.

YELLOW

YOU NOW Your good health and happiness radiate through your aura. Vibrant, mentally agile and alert, you make a wonderful impression wherever you go. There is a sense of playfulness in everything you do. You're like a child, enthusiastic about every person you meet, spontaneous and excited about life, and curious to know exactly what's going on in the world.

FEELINGS You feel light-hearted and carefree – there's no time now for sadness or melancholy. You're more interested in having a good time than worrying about your emotional needs. Anything that excites you or makes you laugh will keep you buzzing with spirit all day long.

THOUGHTS Your mind is in a spin of different ideas and thoughts. You are currently sorting out your priorities and focusing on changing your direction or plans in life. Your thinking is inspired and witty, and you adore phone calls and communicating on all levels.

LIFESTYLE You'll be making new friends and social contacts, generally dazzling and stimulating those around you with your sparkling vitality. Physical exercise is important for you now to let off steam and channel your excess energy.

CAREER Work will seem like a playground; your ambitions will now be creative and light-hearted manoeuvres, rather than serious burdens you fear. Your fun-loving attitude is contagious, and colleagues and employers will love the way you are sharp-witted and on the ball in every project or transaction.

HEALTH Play healthy – go for long walks, get plenty of fresh air or play a competitive sport. Take up a new relaxation technique, such as yoga or t'ai chi, in between bouts of energy expenditure to balance your racy and energetic vitality with moments of silence and stillness.

RED

YOU NOW You're at your peak of passionate energy and fiery enthusiasm for both life and love. You have a powerful ego and feel the need to be an extrovert living on the edge of excitement. Everything you do or say will be done with great belief and integrity. You're so ecstatic about all your friends and relationships that you are driven to tell everyone about your future plans and dreams.

FEELINGS There's no time to analyse your feelings, you just let them flow. You are feeling sensual, sexy and passionate about everything you do. All your feelings are engaged, and you'll experience moments of complete elation.

THOUGHTS You are focused on the present moment, yesterday is unimportant and tomorrow seems a long way ahead. You are impatient, but motivated, and your dynamic mind will be working overtime to enable you to get where you want to be.

LIFESTYLE You barely have time to even take a moment's break, rushing around in a whirl of social engagements, family gatherings or work commitments. You are full of energy and drive. Passion is your motivating force now — if you are in a relationship you're wild about sex; if you're single you'll be thrilled by every possible romantic escapade.

CAREER Your dynamic and charismatic personality won't go unnoticed by those around you. You seem able to do twice as much work as anyone else, and you are geared to maximising your success. You will be able to get any new venture off the ground without hesitation, feeling positively radiant and brimming with achievement in the process.

HEALTH You are in tiptop form, but take care you don't over-exert yourself. A good night's sleep is imperative for you now, so ensure you really allow yourself time for bed. With such passion for life, you won't feel exhausted, but your body may suffer without your being aware of it. Try to set aside at least an hour or two each week, preferably in one session, to devote to pure relaxation.

PINK

YOU NOW Not only are you glowing with compassion and love, but you are also loyal, committed and true to your own self-development. This is a time when you are eager to give of yourself, but have the conviction to know that you have found your true vocation. Love is definitely important for you – if you're not actually in love, you will be sharing good times with as many friends and colleagues as you can. Your warm nature inspires happiness in all around you.

FEELINGS Warm and tender, you care for others whether they are close to you or not. You will feel deeply happy in certain company and are totally filled with longings, desires and dreams about your loved one.

THOUGHTS You are concentrating on your future happiness, and sparkling, imaginative and loving thoughts dominate. You will either be thinking about how to make your love life blissful or you'll be so wrapped up in thinking about your lover you won't have time for anything else to enter your mind.

LIFESTYLE This is a time for social interaction and sharing your loving nature. Alternatively, you could be so deeply in love that togetherness means just the two of you. For you, love encapsulates romance, family happiness or just the simple pleasures in life.

CAREER You are certain about your future role, happy with your vocation. Whatever opportunities come your way will be seen as invaluable to furthering your career. You are charming and delightful, and your commitment to work in the office will be contagious.

HEALTH Although you feel relaxed and content with yourself, this is a time when you need to take more exercise and boost your energy levels. Sometimes too much loving, nurturing and giving can drain your vitality, so make sure you keep equilibrium by embarking on a fitness programme of your choice.

CHAPTER FIVE
AURAS AND RELATIONSHIPS

So how do auras work in relationships? Almost everyone falls in love at some stage or has feelings of warmth and tenderness for another person. But the colours pink and red, which reflect love, sex and intimate relationships, may not appear in their aura or, if they do, another colour such as yellow or blue might be more powerful or dominant. Obviously this doesn't mean that these people are not experiencing or expressing love, it just means that their personality is geared towards expressing love in a different way. For example, if someone has a mostly green aura then their sense of love is basically earthy, sensual and demanding.

Above: Your aura may indicate the type of
person you are usually attracted to.

To find out the way you, your friend or partner expresses or experiences love, use the sense test method in chapter four (see pages 80–81 for how to get started). As well as reading the colour profiles on pages 92–101, read the following descriptions of the love colours. These will give you a very basic and general idea of what kind of lover or intimate relationship you can expect when these colours are powerful in the aura. Remember, the aura changes as you and your circumstances change. Many people have several combinations of colours vibrating at any one time, so a combination of love expressions may have to be interpreted, but don't forget that the dominant colour always expresses the most powerful energy.

WHAT ARE YOU LOOKING FOR?

How often have you picked a partner or lover who is very different from you on the surface, with qualities that are totally opposite to your own? This is because you are often not aware that precisely the opposite characteristics you find so attractive in others are parts of yourself that you have not developed or not yet consciously accepted. You are basically looking for yourself in the eyes, personality and reflection of other people.

So, Joe Bloggs loves Jane because she appears so volatile and creative, while Joe thinks of himself as logical and reliable. In fact, Joe does have a volatile, creative side, but hasn't connected to it yet and instead projects it totally on to Jane. This kind of opposites attract phenomenon happens all the time. It is essentially a

way of discovering who you are and what your values and needs are; unfortunately, it can often hurt when the other person is not able to live up to the image you have of them.

Alternatively, you may find that you are constantly attracted to people who are very like yourself. You feel safe with the 'devil' you know, but it can lead to problems if you aren't ready to accept you have your shadowy sides, too. You are often more aware of some less positive characteristics in others than you are in yourself.

If you look at the compatibilities between the basic colours (pages 106–125), you will see how some combinations are diametrically opposed, creating dynamic, powerful or complex relationships. Relationships between people with auric colours that have a natural affinity are usually calmer, more thoughtful or friendly encounters
– on the surface at least. The compatibilities are arranged according to the woman's basic auric colour, matched with each of the ten basic auric colours for the man. If you are a man, look up under the basic auric colour of your partner and then read the relevant combination.

Check out your own compatibility rating, but don't forget that these are only generalised basic colours. If you have more than one colour predominant in the aura at any given time you

Opposites tend to attract – you are often drawn to someone unlike you because of certain qualities in you that need expressing.

THE TEN BASIC LOVE COLOURS

VIOLET

You love to daydream and fantasise about your partner or just to imagine what it would be like to be in love with someone you haven't even met. Once involved in an intimate relationship, you take a long time to trust and share your feelings with another. Love and sex go hand in hand for you, so you need a partner who understands your wildest dreams.

LAVENDER

You fear rejection, so your light, flirtatious side hides a deep vulnerability. Your imagination knows no bounds and you're ready for complete sexual fulfilment as long as it's a magical, gentle and caring relationship. If your partner is stressed, you'll feel it deeply, but on the surface you'll delight and tease, flirt and enjoy taking pleasure whenever you can.

TURQUOISE

You love a tranquil, easy-going relationship, in which you can feel relaxed and inspired by your lover. Beauty, humour and intellectual interaction are essential to you. Falling in love with the idea of love before you've got to know your partner means you are initially idealistic but then dispirited if your expectations aren't met.

BLUE

You need an intimate and highly creative relationship, in which both of you communicate and share your lives totally. You're so sensitive to your partner's needs that you often forget your own. Emotionally you feel blissful in a calm, creative environment; sexually you enjoy deeply intimate moments, when you can express total sensual pleasure.

AQUAMARINE

Your feelings are often a frustration for you, so a relationship based on intellectual fascination, fun and good humour is essential to prevent you from becoming restless. Getting bogged down in emotions isn't for you; freedom is, though, and sex can be outrageous and wild. You're very in tune with your partner and want to give them pleasure, as long as they don't make demands on you.

DEEP GREEN

You have an earthy, practical attitude towards your relationships. Sex is for sensual pleasure and fun, and your feelings are often hidden from view. You are loyal and ambitious for the future of any partnership and will try hard to make it work. Your enthusiasm for making a success of your relationships means that you often do. You're more likely to remain with one partner for longer than people with any other colour dominant in the aura.

ORANGE

You need loads of freedom and space if a relationship is to survive. Usually extrovert and fun to have around, you love sex for the sake of sex and don't let yourself get too emotionally involved. You need a relationship in which you can have frequent periods apart. You love adventurous relationships, and a fling or affair keeps you inspired.

YELLOW

You prefer intimate conversations to sexual gymnastics. Your mind is eager for amusement or challenge from your partner, rather than deep emotions, complex feelings and moods. You're light-hearted, flirtatious and unpossessive and prefer a partner who can match your wit and humour to one who is only good in bed.

RED

You adore sex, and physical fun is the most important part of a relationship. You have loads of energy and passion, so you need an equally demanding partner who can match and keep up with your extreme moods. They must be as passionate and dynamic about love and sex as you are. Bliss is to take your partner to the heights of sexual pleasure.

PINK

You love the high of being in love, of the first romantic yearnings and wishes, hopes and dreams. You are tender and caring and need a partner who can be as romantic and sexually creative as you. Infatuation with many people means you take a long time to get really close to just one other person.

WHO'S COMPATIBLE WITH WHOM? VIOLET

Violet woman/Violet man

They drift around in a haze of dreams and fantasies. They have a wonderful ethereal rapport, which means they are almost telepathic. When apart, they both feel as if they've lost their soulmate, so they can become very dependent on each other. This is a dreamy and intimate relationship, in which the unexpected often happens simply because they become so involved in their personal world that they lose all track of time.

Violet woman/Lavender man

As long as he remembers to indulge her in her fantasy world, this is an easy-going relationship. She longs for complete intimacy, and he'll share most of her dreams, except when he's feeling in a flirtatious mood. She is serious about sex and love; he's serious about having more fun.

Violet woman/Turquoise man

Both love harmony and blissful sex, although her wilder sexual fantasies may unnerve him. He wants an easy-going and peaceful existence; she might be reticent about sharing her feelings initially. They may be unable to make joint decisions because they often can't agree, but they'll adore sharing beautiful and magical moments instead.

Violet woman/Blue man

He is totally sensitive to her every need and emotion, but he feels too restricted by her tendency to escape into her imagination instead of facing the reality of life. She loves his sensual style. She also needs to remind him to make his own choices and not to rely on her to do so when he's in one of his confused moods.

Violet woman/Aquamarine man

This relationship could provide a few fireworks. She loves dreaming; he prefers to communicate and analyse every situation. Her imagination and mystique, as well as her unpredictable behaviour, keep him drawn to her, though. He may hang around as long as he gets enough freedom.

Violet woman/Deep green man

She may find him too practical and sensible for her own dreamy nature. He enjoys sex and takes great pleasure in indulging her every whim, but he won't be so fond of displaying his feelings. However, she needs to feel protected and nurtured, and this might be enough to prompt him to stay to show how loyal he really is.

Violet woman/Orange man

These two are very different in their approach to love and life. He wants sex and adventure, no ties and loads of space. She wants commitment and a dreamy look in his eye. He may give her the look, but only if she expects no promises. He's fascinated by her glamorous allure, however, so it could be a case of opposites colliding for a sexual fling.

Violet woman/Yellow man

She'll be amused by his conversation and charm, and he'll adore her imagination. However, he's too fickle and outrageously flirtatious, which she may find spoils every party. He adores facts; she prefers fiction. He wants to network and have a wild social life, whereas she would prefer to escape into films, or her head.

Violet woman/Red man

A powerful magnetic attraction exists between these two, but it may be short-lived. He's passionate about her mysterious beauty and adores her wicked fantasies. She wants discreet intimacy, laced with erotic pleasure; he wants it too, but he craves to be challenged, even dominated, above all. Their surface differences are likely to create havoc when they are not fulfilling the physical side of their relationship.

Violet woman/Pink man

This relationship seems idyllic on the surface as he adores her mystery and glamour, and she's touched by his knight-in-shining-armour appeal and romantic approach. However, neither can make straightforward decisions so they may drift along in a haze of 'being in love' until life starts to make practical demands on them, and neither can cope.

LAVENDER

Lavender woman/Lavender man

They're both so insecure they want life to be light-hearted and pleasurable. All kinds of mental and physical games keep them amused. They are not keen on showing their feelings in the height of sexual passion, but they can express their gentle attitude to love without feeling under the spotlight. Together, they will be stimulating company for each other.

Lavender woman/Turquoise man

On the surface this is a fun-loving and sexually fulfilling relationship, a good combination for carefree companionship. However, she will be aware of his high expectations, which she may find difficult to live up to after a while. He wants perfection and beauty, and would do well to recognise that she probably comes closer than many to such an ideal.

Lavender woman/Blue man

These two exude a cosy, intimate energy when they are together. He knows how deeply vulnerable she is and is sensitive to her changing moods. She loves his sexual tenderness and feels comfortable with his calm artistic temperament. Both can fall in love and stay there more easily than fall out of it.

Lavender woman/Aquamarine man

To begin with he will give utter pleasure and seem totally compatible with her gentle, sensitive nature. Yet he really needs a relationship in which his mind is challenged and active. She may prefer him to be more aware of her feelings and may become jealous of his need for personal freedom.

Lavender woman/Deep green man

She'll adore his bear hugs and pleasure-seeking sense of fun, but she may not be able to keep up with his ambitious and motivated side. He loves planning and organising the relationship and, although she loves to go with the flow, she may tire of his constant need to plot every moment of their togetherness.

Lavender woman/Orange man

He adores her gentle, light-hearted and sometimes frivolous approach to life, but he may find her more vulnerable side less attractive. He wants a woman who can support his career, give him space; she wants a man who will commit himself. They may clash when it comes to the serious aspects of their relationship.

Lavender woman/Yellow man

She loves his easy-going approach to life, and he finds her light-hearted and sexually fun. However, if she reveals how sensitive she is behind her extrovert façade he may become uneasy in her presence. She needs someone who truly cares, and he likes to feel care-free. Sexually they are good companions, but they'll need to work to make it long lasting.

Lavender woman/Red man

This relationship is not for the faint-hearted. He's steaming with passion for someone so apparently fragile and beautiful, but he may get a shock when he discovers she is very needy. She'll be fascinated at first by his dynamic vitality, but she may cool off when she discovers his own fast-paced lifestyle comes first.

Lavender woman/Pink man

They'll drift in a cloud of mutual vagueness. He'll be so in love with her magical allure he won't notice what day it is; she, for her part, wants commitment before she's ready to share herself, and his blatant infatuation with her means she warms to him more quickly than to many. This will not be a long-lasting relationship if he's only high on love and not her.

Lavender woman/Violet man

A wonderful rapport exists between these two, which is often long lasting. He's deeply sexual, and she loves sharing his wildest dreams. She can inspire him with her light-heartedness and beauty, and he gives her the feeling that they've met somewhere before. This is a dreamy connection, as long as they both honour their deeper spiritual world.

TURQUOISE

Turquoise woman/Turquoise man

They can become utterly dependent on each other, with a feeling of real tenderness. Neither has much drive or motivation, so they may spend days trying to make any real decisions or plans. They prefer this rather casual approach, since it keeps them both carefree and noncommittal and ensures they always come back for more.

Turquoise woman/Blue man

This can be a relationship made in heaven. He adores exchanging words and physical pleasure. He also loves creating new opportunities for change within the relationship, so she will enjoy his inspiring thoughts and sensitive feelings. She wants complete harmony and a peaceful lifestyle, and in this sense he comes closest to her ideal man.

Turquoise woman/Aquamarine man

This has the potential to be a wonderful relationship if he can accept that she needs to know what part she plays in his life, especially the physical side. He can be awkward and resist commitment, which she tolerates for a while. However, she has many dreams for the future, and – although he genuinely admires them – they may not fit in with his plans to remain footloose and fancy-free.

Turquoise woman/Deep green man

Although these two are very different in their approach to life, they can easily establish a long-lasting relationship. She may find his practical vision and common sense of great value in bringing her down to earth occasionally. They both love sensual pleasure and together enjoy a fabulous physical rapport. The only niggle may be her need for a more tranquil relationship that moves at its own pace, whereas he's ambitious for one that is more planned and going somewhere.

Turquoise woman/Orange man

Both are carefree to begin with, but her heart is softer and she needs more tender loving care than this man can give her. Her idealistic view of love means she's attracted by his gregarious charm and winning smile. He's so much more extrovert than she is but their sexual rapport is stunning.

Turquoise woman/Yellow man

He sees her as absolutely feminine and charming, but his restlessness means he won't be around for long if she can't amuse him over a candlelit dinner. He needs intellectual stimulation and an extrovert lifestyle first, sexual excitement second. She prefers the romantic and heady bliss of love, rather than a challenging evening out playing poker.

Turquoise woman/Red man

A powerful attraction exists between these two. He's fascinated by her tranquil nature and longs to show her how dynamic and fiery he is. She's equally excited by his passionate and impulsive desire for her and imagines him as a perfect lover to take her to the outer limits of pleasure. However, he wants to be the boss and she would rather they were equal.

Turquoise woman/Pink man

They are both laid back and easily led astray by each other's emotions. She finds him seriously romantic, which keeps her fascinated. He adores her tranquil approach to life, but neither of them can ever get on with the practicalities of the relationship. Both will dream about different things: she about him moving in; he about keeping things the way they were when they first met. This is a sexually magnetic, but potentially confusing, relationship.

Turquoise woman/Violet man

He takes a long time to trust her, but once their intimacy is established they have a fabulous rapport. The only problem is he loves to imagine and fantasise about life, while she would rather talk seriously about it. If he opens up and shares his dreams, then their sexual and intellectual capacity for happiness is assured.

Turquoise woman/Lavender man

He wants a light, easy-going relationship, so does she but her expectations are higher. He loves her sense of humour and she enjoys his funny phone calls and laid-back attitude to life. When the crunch comes he's not prepared to commit himself, and the relationship is likely to fizzle out, like so many others before.

BLUE

Blue woman/Blue man

It takes a long time for closeness to develop because each is very cautious of the other. They're both so sensitive that when they finally create an intimate and sensually rewarding relationship each will have an intuitive sense of what the other wants and needs. They are highly private and secretive, so won't be going out much. A long-term commitment is necessary for both of them.

Blue woman/Aquamarine man

She is sensitive to his every change of mood, and he prefers to avoid his feelings so he may begin to feel trapped by her more serious side. However, they have a wonderful sexual rapport as he loves to give her pleasure, and she responds with a deeply intuitive sense of what he wants in return. This partnership is not good for long-term commitment, but is wonderful for sexual bliss.

Blue woman/Deep green man

These two are very attracted by each other's differences. He's protective, ambitious and practical; she's moody, changeable and impractical. This can be a very supportive relationship, as long as she learns to live with his need for success. She may feel lonely when he's constantly on the phone to business associates, so unless she can communicate her fears the initial passion may not last.

Blue woman/Orange man

This relationship has the potential to be either totally disastrous or completely fascinating. She craves physical bliss and he'll certainly give her the greatest of pleasure, but he won't give up his freedom. His extrovert nature is initially a powerful attraction and she adores his terrific energy and crazy lifestyle. However, he won't be keen to commit himself to her gentle ways and needs. This combination is wonderful for a fling, but needs a lot of work for anything more.

Blue woman/Yellow man

On the surface there is an excellent rapport between these two, as they are each able to stimulate the other's need for intellectual communication. The more cerebral the relationship, the better for him, but she would prefer more physical and emotional interaction. As long as she isn't possessive or jealous, they can have a good future; and as long as he truly adores her, she'll be loyal and fun-loving.

Blue woman/Red man

This is possibly one of the most erotic matches. He's fiery, passionate and ready for sex every minute of the day; she's cool, glamorous, aloof and mysterious. He's riveted by her mystery and she's fascinated by his libido. Together their sexual rapport is fabulous. Their only possible problem is that she may not provide enough of a challenge for his impulsive and egotistic nature.

Blue woman/Pink man

She adores his romantic and caring attitude, but she may crave a more interactive relationship than he currently offers. Red roses and romantic dinners are all very well, but she needs more than tenderness. He may never get close enough to truly know her – the problem is that she finds it very hard to open up, and he's so wrapped up in being in love he won't even want her to.

Blue woman/Violet man

These two have a wonderful, physically exciting relationship. Sensually they have a tremendous rapport and his imagination knows no bounds with her. She adores his unpredictable behaviour and changing moods, and he's enchanted by her cool glamour and mysterious charm. This could be a relationship that survives longer than most simply because they won't have time for anyone else in their lives.

Blue woman/ Lavender man

She can see through his often flirtatious side and understands exactly how vulnerable he really is. However, he won't want to admit to this for a long time, until he's really sure she's as compassionate and adoring as she seems. There is a fantastic sexual rapport between them: he's magical and inventive; she's sensual and warm.

Blue woman/Turquoise man

He adores her glamour and cool mysterious sexuality. He may, however, make too many assumptions about her, almost putting her on a pedestal, for her to sustain such a perfectly wonderful image. This could be the kind of relationship she's looking for as long as she keeps her feelings out of the equation. He loves a laugh and good conversation; she does too, but only if it leads somewhere.

AQUAMARINE

Aquamarine woman/Aquamarine man

This is a fun-loving relationship, with few ties or commitments. Both want freedom and can be extremely devoted to each other, as long as they both have an equal share of personal space. They enjoy the lighter aspects of life and so can relax together, knowing emotional conflicts won't arise. Sexually they are dynamite, but if either gets bored they may drift away to something more fascinating.

Aquamarine woman/Deep green man

This is a good combination if she has a career and ambitions, as this man certainly adores success and achievement. She may find he's too serious, but his earthy sexuality sends her wild. His common sense tells him she needs her space and he won't interfere if she wants to see her other friends. Although not obviously passionate on the surface, this relationship certainly has the potential to be a long-term success.

Aquamarine woman/Orange man

These two make a stunning couple – both are extrovert and lively, but both are likely to get led astray if the mood takes them. Sexually they transport each other to giddy heights, and his love of adventure drives her wild. She may be too sensitive at times to his rather flirtatious and 'lover of all women' approach. They are likely to stick together, just because each is as stubborn as the other.

Aquamarine woman/Yellow man

She adores his intellectualising and airy approach to life. He finds her easy to be with and relaxes enough to indulge in erotic phone calls and a fun-loving approach to sex. Both need their space and to feel unpossessed, but because they are both so lightweight in their approach to intimacy they can easily get confused about how close they actually are.

Aquamarine woman/Red man

He's hot and she's cool, so a tremendous magnetism exists between them. Sexually they are inspiring and creative. He'll never run out of energy and desire, but he may prefer her to be more demanding or dominant at times. Her need for space means he can feel left out in the cold, but if they can keep their heads, this could be a powerful attraction that won't burn out.

Aquamarine woman/Pink man

As long as he remains romantic and spontaneous, she'll adore him. She wants outrageous fun, but he may not be able to keep up with her less emotional way of loving. If he starts to go weak at the knees she may give him up for someone less besotted. She adores romance, but hates to see weakness because she knows what it is to feel vulnerable.

Aquamarine woman/Violet man

He's a dreamer; she's more practical and needs a partner who can share her sense of enthusiasm for sex and life. Initially he will fascinate her, but once she realises he lives in a fantasy world and can be too serious about life, she may retreat to her own space. Sexually they could have perfect pleasure, but she may begin to feel trapped in his irresistible but possessive arms.

Aquamarine woman/Lavender man

This could be a magical relationship, as long as he respects her need for space. She loves his light-hearted easy-going attitude to love, and together they enjoy intellectual fun and social whirls to keep them alive and buzzing. Sexually he may not be as dynamic as she might like, but if he keeps her laughing they'll certainly be friends for life.

Aquamarine woman/Turquoise man

These two are very similar, but very different. Both love an easy-going and unemotional relationship, but she's a free spirit, and he's tied to his own search for perfection. They may have fun for a while, but their quests in life are different and neither will be able to feel comfortable in the other's arms for long.

Aquamarine woman/Blue man

She may find him too possessive and sensitive. If he reveals his feelings too soon she may panic. Intimacy between them is erotic and sustainable, but the world of emotions is too heavy for her airy approach to love. He may fall desperately in love with her free-spirited lifestyle, but he won't be able to match her stamina for pleasure and social sophistication.

DEEP GREEN

Deep green woman/Deep green man

Essentially these two make a perfect couple on the surface. Both are pragmatic, down-to-earth and supreme sensualists. However, they are also both ambitious, sometimes ruthless and always stubborn. This means that if their lifestyles clash or they move in different circles they may land up going their separate ways.

Deep green woman/Orange man

This is a practical relationship, which works best if she's ambitious and independent and they live separately so that he can have the space he needs. He adores her sensual earthiness and they'll have great sexual fun together. She enjoys his fun-loving attitude, which takes her away from the stress of her busy life. They will have a good rapport, both mentally and sexually.

Deep green woman/Yellow man

She'll adore his gregarious nature and be inspired by his wit and charm. This could be a stable and long-lasting relationship, as both prefer action and pleasure rather than deep feelings and ego battles. He's fascinated by her strong ambitions and respects her need for power.

Deep green woman/Red man

Neither has time to indulge in emotion, and both love pleasure for the sake of pleasure. This could be a fabulous long-lasting relationship if they can find the time to get together. She can keep up with his sexual impulsiveness, but he may find it harder to keep up with her serious attitude to work.

Deep green woman/Pink man

She's fascinated by his romantic and tender feelings, but may feel trapped if he's too compliant and compromising. She prefers a good debate to a dreamy walk in the woods, and he could fall head over heels in love with her powerful, independent nature. This could be a difficult relationship, unless she enjoys achieving goddess status in his eyes.

Deep green woman/Violet man

He's totally in awe of her pragmatic and highly motivated nature, and she may be equally spellbound by his mysterious and secretive approach to life. Mentally they have little in common, but physically they could stir great ripples of passion and earthy sensual love, as long as he doesn't expect her to reveal her feelings.

Deep green woman/Lavender man

She will be flattered by his attention, but may find him too whimsical, scatty and moody for her own more sophisticated needs. Sexually this could be a fun, light-hearted and genuine friendship rather than passionate love. There's no animal magnetism here, but it could be good for a fling.

Deep green woman/Turquoise man

There is a wonderful rapport on the surface, since neither really likes to express their feelings or get emotional. His idealism is the only problem, for she is so down-to-earth he might find it hard to deal with the fact she is a woman not a goddess. However, it could be a sensually stimulating relationship, as long as he learns to take her as he finds her.

Deep green woman/Blue man

They could initially be fascinated by each other's very different attitudes to life. The relationship is definitely sexually inspiring, but not easy as a long-term commitment. He's too sensitive and needs to feel totally involved, whereas she would rather socialise and make an impression in all the right places.

Deep green woman/Aquamarine man

These two have a great rapport, both mentally and physically. Neither likes to reveal their emotional needs, and both prefer sex to be pleasurable, sensual and erotic. He'll give her more pleasure than she could dream of, and she'll remind him that good fun and a sense of humour are what inspires him to love her.

ORANGE

Orange woman/Orange man

If they can both respect each other's need for freedom and space, there is great potential here. This is probably the only combination in which a couple could develop a totally unconditional relationship based on trust. Both are light-hearted and flirtatious, and as long as neither of them has a touch of blue in their aura they won't get jealous or possessive. Although unconventional, this could be a long-lasting relationship.

Orange woman/Yellow man

At first they'll be spellbound by their wit and humour. However, she needs lots of outrageous sex, and he prefers talking about it. This could be great if he can develop a more physical attitude to his erotic thoughts, and if she can learn to enjoy his intellectual approach to love and sex as well as his agile body.

Orange woman/Red man

This is dynamite sexually – a free and easy relationship, physically passionate and mentally exciting. However, she needs more space than he usually likes to give, and so they could indulge in passionate games of hide-and-seek. She will do most of the hiding and he'll end up doing most of the seeking if he gets too possessive and demanding.

Orange woman/Pink man

She may find him irresistible when they first meet, but may quickly tire of his undying love routines or phone calls at all hours of the day and night. He needs gentleness and warmth; she needs humour and a footloose and fancy-free attitude. This could be a sexy relationship, but the long-term prospects are not good.

Orange woman/Violet man

He may be too serious when they first meet, but she may be drawn to him by his hypnotic and powerful gaze. Opposites definitely attract and there's a tremendous surge of desire for each other, resulting in a deeply satisfying sexual relationship. Mentally, however, he's too intense for her, and she's too free-spirited and independent for him.

Orange woman/Lavender man

Initially there is a fabulous physical rapport between these two, since they are both lively, flirtatious and good-humoured. However, he may begin to feel insecure when she demands more space and freedom, and she may feel trapped by a hunch that underneath that vibrant charisma he's got deep, intense feelings. As a long-term relationship it could prove painful for both of them.

Orange woman/Turquoise man

He'll adore her from the moment he sets eyes on her. Her vivacious and extrovert personality makes him urgent with desire, and she loves his mind and his body with passion. If he can accept her independent spirit and fairly laid-back approach, he may stick around in her heart for longer than she thought.

Orange woman/Blue man

He will be drawn by her versatile and sometimes inconsistent sexuality. She may tease him and enjoy the game. Physically they may find each other compelling and totally awesome, but their mental and emotional needs are so different. The relationship could be dramatic for a while, but she needs more space than he is willing to give.

Orange woman/Aquamarine man

Both are adaptable and can work out any problems simply by forgetting about them. They both enjoy sex for the sake of sex and share the same attitude towards commitment and emotional entanglements. They could have a long-lasting rapport if each is strong enough to accept the other's need for freedom, adventure and space at all costs.

Orange woman/Deep green man

This has the potential to be a lovely partnership if he's the ambitious type and she's the successful career woman. Both are trusting, and she adores his sensual, earthy approach to sex. He admires her independent streak and won't try to trap her. She may be more fickle and extrovert than he is, but she'll feel relaxed in his company.

YELLOW

Yellow woman/Yellow man

This is a very entertaining relationship, but there's always a danger it may collapse. Although they are both lively, amusing and intellectually matched, both like to do their own thing and may go their separate ways too soon. They have an easy-going rapport – they'll argue to the bitter end about all manner of subjects, but never row about the relationship.

Yellow woman/Red man

To begin with, this is a passionate and inspiring relationship. However, she needs a light approach to lovemaking, while he can be demanding and passionate in the extreme. She enjoys his busy nature and he'll tolerate her restlessness. This is a stimulating relationship, but probably short-lived.

Yellow woman/Pink man

With long candlelit dinners, music and wine, this could be a romantic partnership. Both love talking, and conversations will be sexy and fun. Neither wants to get too dependent on the other and this detached approach keeps the relationship gentle and warm. She may get bored, however, if his romantic mood doesn't change to something more mentally challenging.

Yellow woman/Violet man

This is one of those classic love-hate relationships – both are fascinated by their opposite attitudes to life. She'll be frustrated by his secrecy, but adore his imagination; he'll find her frivolous nature unbearable, but love her mental agility. However, this kind of friction makes for a sexy relationship, so they may last longer than either expects.

Yellow woman/Lavender man

As long as he can keep his feelings to himself, this could be a fun-loving and happy relationship. Both like to flirt and enjoy a good social life, so they won't get bored with each other. Sexually it will be good fun, rather than passionate and intense – these two make good companions, rather than deeply intimate lovers.

Yellow woman/Turquoise man

He has such high ideals, and she may initially fill every one of them because she is good at playing any role. Both prefer the idea of love rather than the experience of it. They are excellent when they're out socialising, but often become bored when they are alone. This is a friendly, sexually magical relationship, but if a crisis occurs there's a chance they may part, as neither is good at dealing with the practicalities of life.

Yellow woman/Blue man

His sensitivity contrasts sharply with her carefree attitude to life. They could have fun communicating, sharing the good times and generally having a fling, but their needs are so different that they may find it a struggle to maintain a deeper relationship, which he needs and she finds too claustrophobic. This is good for fun, not so good for long-term commitment.

Yellow woman/Aquamarine man

Although an unconventional couple, these two have an exciting, inspiring and good-humoured relationship. There's a magical quality to their sexual wildness and they both love to gossip, chatter and amuse each other. They rarely get bored and are both adaptable, keen to be on the go all the time. He adores her wit and charm, while she is fascinated by his cool glamour and need for freedom.

Yellow woman/Deep green man

She loves variety and is versatile and charming in company, so he may find her totally irresistible. Yet he prefers routines and an earthier existence than she does so they may come to blows unless she can adapt enough to his energy flow. Sexually he is more interested in the sensual aspects of lovemaking, while she prefers to talk about sex and keep it light and entertaining.

Yellow woman/Orange man

This is a highly stimulating and sexually honest relationship. Both need space and freedom, and if he disappears for a few weeks to the wilds of Alaska she won't be alarmed. He adores her wit and good humour; she loves his honest, free spirit. What keeps the two of them together is their mutual need for an unconventional relationship with no emotional ties.

RED

Red woman/Red man

These two are competitive and high-spirited, so their relationship will be like a raging inferno and sexually dynamic. Both need to express their passion, and they'll have momentary flashes of temper too. If they fight, they often end up in each other's arms. They are both fiery and spontaneous, but likely to go their separate ways peacefully after the flames have died down.

Red woman/Pink man

She adores his romantic and creative style of loving. She's passionate about his gentle sexuality, and if he likes her to play a dominant role she'll gladly do so. However, she needs energy and spirit, and he may be too passive and idealistic for her demanding sexual hunger.

Red woman/Violet man

Although these two have very different approaches to sex, there is a magnetic and powerful attraction between them. It can be an enriching experience, but she can't get to grips with his inner world of feeling and imagination, and he finds it difficult to understand her more impatient and volatile moods and rages of passion. There is potential for a long-term relationship, but it will be full of chaos.

Red woman/Lavender man

To begin with she loves his flirtatious and funny nature, but if she sees through this defensiveness she may begin to feel uncomfortable with his more needy side. Passion abounds, so sexually this is an easy-going and lively relationship. As for a long-term commitment, they are liable to be tempted by others too soon.

Red woman/Turquoise man

She drives him wild with desire, and he easily adapts to her dynamic sexual nature. However, his need for tranquillity and a cooler, less raging relationship will quickly make him wonder if he can keep up with her stamina; she enjoys his company, but never quite feels he's motivated enough to keep up with her pace.

Red woman/Blue man

These two have a sexy rapport, although they are both so different in temperament. She needs sex on demand; he can supply it but may prefer to spend more time in peaceful harmony, rather than trail-blazing round every social function. Together they can achieve physical pleasure, but she hates his possessiveness and he won't give up his need for total commitment.

Red woman/Aquamarine man

Neither is possessive and neither wants to be committed, so this makes for an excellent, dynamic relationship. However, he wants intellectual friendship and she prefers physical communication, the venting of feelings, passion and sexual fire. He loves her powerful sex drive, but may at times feel driven to despair!

Red woman/Deep green man

These two are very different, but the prospects are excellent if they are both ambitious. He's practical and down-to-earth, and she adores his sensual sexuality. He loves her passion, but may find her too impetuous and ready to take risks he would rather not. They are likely to have lots of verbal battles, but can make a formidable partnership.

Red woman/Orange man

They have a superb rapport, as long as she doesn't get jealous when he's not around. He needs more freedom than she does, which could cause problems, but their mutual passion is undeniable. If they have the same aims and approach to an independent lifestyle, this could be an exciting but unusual relationship.

Red woman/Yellow man

This can be a stimulating and lively partnership, but they will find they don't have much in common once the initial rush of passion wears off. He needs mental exercise, she physical. However, they never resent each other's differences and will probably stay good friends for life.

PINK

Pink woman/Pink man
Both are totally in love from the first moment and probably won't even know why – the ultimate in romance. They will dream the same dreams, share the same magical moments, and talk long into the night about their future plans and schemes. However, the reality and practical side of having a relationship may prove to be their undoing.

Pink woman/Violet man
She adores his imaginative lovemaking, and he's passionate about her dreamy and tender romantic side. In a way they can both indulge in their wildest fantasies, and he's probably the one who can keep up this imaginary world longer than anyone else can. The only things missing are adaptability and realism.

Pink woman/Lavender man
These two are made for a creative and inspiring love affair, although not necessarily a long-term dream. She won't ever get close to him, and he wouldn't let her anyway. In a way the idealistic vision they have of each other is what will keep them together. This is not a particularly sexy relationship, but a highly romantic one.

Pink woman/Turquoise man
They will have a beautiful and idealistic love affair, in which both are so infatuated they cannot bear to separate. Neither has a great deal of drive or motivation about the future so they may never make any plans – or even reach a decision about which film they'll see. Tender and humorous, they are likely to stay together longer if he doesn't find she has any flaws.

Pink woman/Blue man
He's totally sensitive to her gentle and romantic tenderness, but whether he can truly communicate his feelings to her only he knows. She may listen eagerly, but it is romantic words she wants to hear, not emotional tangles and conflicts in his life. He needs to feel close and intimate; she just needs to feel in love with love.

Pink woman/Aquamarine man

They have a sexy rapport, but it is not likely to last long unless she can give him the space to roam. His sexual style is wilder than hers, and erratic, so she may get frustrated when he doesn't show up on that special date. Both have different needs, so this combination can be excellent for a fling, but romantic commitment isn't in his nature.

Pink woman/Deep green man

She makes him feel like a knight in shining armour, and he makes her feel like a princess. Together they have a sensual rapport that is full of passion. She adores his down-to-earth approach, and he's entranced by her almost boundless tenderness. If they can truly enjoy the balance of such opposite energies this could be a long-lasting and peaceful relationship.

Pink woman/Orange man

There is not only a clash of colours here, but also a clash of motivation. He is extrovert and social and wants sex for the fun of it; she wants to fall into a partnership and spend every night alone with him. They could have a sexy exchange of very different energies for a while, but the relationship is not likely to last unless she has a streak of orange in her aura.

Pink woman/Yellow man

On the surface this is a light-hearted and harmonious relationship, neither ruffled nor too bound up in emotional intensity. However, he may be too jokey and fun-loving for her, and she may be too serious and gentle for him. He needs challenge, and she needs togetherness. This is not an easy combination, but they could have a warm-hearted affair for a while.

Pink woman/Red man

This could just work if he's prepared to keep romance high on the list of priorities. He may be too impulsive, but she'll find his passion keeps her romantically amused. However, she may not be able to keep up with his spontaneous and exaggerated moods, no matter how much she thinks she loves him.

INDEX

PICTURE CREDITS

Pictures copyright ©: e.t. archive: p. 19; Ian Parsons: p. 34; Image Bank: p. 20, 25, 26–7, 29, 31, 40, 89, 95, 96, 97, 100, 101, 102; Images Colour Library: p. 14–15, 21, 22, 24, 28, 32, 33, 38, 83, 84, 85, 88, 89, 90, 93; Photonica: p. 92; Science Photo Library: p. 16, 17; Superstock: p. 28, 103; Tibet Images: p. 18; Tony Stone: p. 10, 12, 13, 23, 30, 35, 36, 37, 42, 43, 44, 45, 46, 80, 82, 83, 86, 87, 94, 98, 99.